The Lord's Prayer in My Life

The Basic Lessons of Prayer

by
Marbury E. Anderson

Kirk House Publishers
Minneapolis, Minnesota

The Lord's Prayer in My Life

The Basic Lessons of Prayer

Library of Congress Cataloging-in-Publication data
Anderson, Marbury E., 1923-
The Lord's Prayer in my life: the basic lessons of prayer/ by Marbury E. Anderson.
p. cm.
ISBN 1-886513-23-6
1. Lord's prayer—Meditations. I. Title.
BV230 .A66 2000
226.9'606—dc21 00-022189

Kirk House Publishers, PO Box 390759, Minneapolis, MN 55439
Manufactured in the United States of America

Contents

The Lord's Prayer

Our Father in heaven,

hallowed be your name,

your kingdom come,

your will be done,
  on earth as in heaven.

Give us today our daily bread.

Forgive us our sins,
  as we forgive those who sin against us.

Save us from the time of trial

and deliver us from evil.

For the kingdom, the power, and the glory are yours,
  now and forever.

Amen.

The Lord's Prayer

Our Father, who art in heaven,

hallowed be thy name,

thy kingdom come,

thy will be done,
  on earth as it is in heaven.

Give us this day our daily bread,

and forgive us our trespasses,
  as we forgive those who trespass against us;

and lead us not into temptation,

but deliver us from evil.

For thine is the kingdom, and the power, and the glory,
  forever and ever.

Amen.

In gratitude for Sylvia, my wife,
who has been my chief partner in prayer
for more than 50 years.

Preface

In a spiritual renaissance prayer becomes the focus as we open our lives to a renewed activity of God—and a renewing relationship with the Almighty.

For generations *The Lord's Prayer* has been a model as children have been taught to pray. While focusing on the mechanics of prayer we may lose sight of dynamics of the relationship to God. But in praying we are drawn into that great communion which is rooted in the heart of God. Prayer is the spiritual connector between God and the people of God and between all of the people of God. It keeps us in touch with ourselves.

Pastor Anderson preached often on *The Lord's Prayer* in his service to five parishes: St. Lukes, Buffalo and Trinity, Sheridan, Wyoming: Grace, Ft. Worth Texas; Messiah, Minneapolis, Minnesota; Augustan, Denver, Colorado; and Grace, Mankato, Minnesota. Through those sermons he came to appreciate the depth of this prayer and determined to share what the prayer had come to mean in his own life. This is a "book filled with the spiritual wisdom and biblical scholarship accumulated by a pastor who knows how to put the 'Sunday world' of our faith in our 'Monday worlds' where we live and work," says Pastor David A Beety of Hope Evangelical Lutheran Church in Minneapolis.

Whether in the "closet" or in those public places where Christians gather, our cry remains, "Lord, teach us to pray." This book will not only give you new insights into *The Lord's Prayer* but will lead you to evaluate your own relationship to God through prayer.

—The Publisher

Introduction

The Lord's Prayer. It has always been a part of my prayer life. When I learned our second son, Marston, was HIV-positive, it became the cornerstone of my prayer life. I found myself praying:

> Marston's Father in heaven, hallow your name in Marston. Your kingdom come to Marston. Your will be done in Marston's life, as it is in heaven. Give Marston your daily bread. Forgive Marston his sins, as he forgives those who sin against him. Save Marston from the time of trial. Deliver Marston from evil. For your kingdom, power, and glory are for Marston now and forever. Amen.

Since that painful and grievous day in 1992 when he died, I have found myself praying the Lord's Prayer in similar manner for other members of my family, for my friends, for congregations in which I have been involved, for communities in which tragedy has struck or in which I have been traveling. If I took the time, it is the way in which daily I would voice my every prayer for those for whom I pray.

The Lord's Prayer. It is the prayer with which I start the day and with which I close it. It is the table prayer before I take the Holy Sacrament. It is the prayer which devotionally unites me with others as I, with them, seek God.

I can identify with the member of Trinity Lutheran Church in Sheridan, Wyoming, who told of the conflict she had had when her doctor prescribed surgery. "Not another surgery," she argued. Then came the night when the pain was so intense. In that night there was one thing that carried her through. It was in praying over and over and over again the Lord's Prayer.

I appreciate the solace and strength of the shut-in of Gustavus Adolphus Lutheran Church in St. Paul, Minnesota. He is lonely. His wife of six decades has died. He yearns for the day he shall be with her. What keeps him going? It is his riding on the shoulders of Jesus praying the Lord's Prayer, the prayer he prays over and over again throughout each day.

The Lord's Prayer. I have come to the conclusion that this prayer is the great cornerstone of all prayer. This prayer is the essence of what my prayer life is all about. This prayer is really where my prayer life begins and ends. It is the prayer upon which my life is built. It is my intent in this book to share with you reflections on the petitions of the prayer, thereby taking you with me into the depths that have opened for me as I have wrestled with its content. It is also my intent to share devotional experiences on each petition which have emerged as I have noted in each petition focus words and thoughts.

I remember reading the account of an elderly Christian who said that, though she had been praying the Lord's Prayer for years, she had just begun to really pray it. She thought of herself as having barely gotten into the first petition. For her the prayer was like a mine whose rich reserves and resources had hardly been touched. There was so much to fathom and contemplate, so much yet to experience and know.

The Lord's Prayer is indeed like that. It is really too much for a single lifetime. It becomes for us a never-ending experience of growth. Every moment in time it is new. Every happening in life brings fresh and vital applications.

The disciples thought to pray, and they felt the need for help. Turning to Jesus they said, "Lord, teach us to pray . . ." (Luke 11:1). They were probably surprised that Jesus responded, "When you pray, say. . . . "Then he proceeded to give them the prayer we have come to know as the Lord's Prayer. Jesus apparently considered this prayer the best possible prayer lesson he could give his disciples. Jesus, who came that we might be in right relationship with God, saw this prayer as helping us into that right relationship. He who called us "to love our neighbor as ourselves" saw this prayer as bringing us also into the best possible relationship with others as well as with ourselves. Jesus gave us this prayer to equip us to face anything and everything that might come our way.

Thus, as I enter into the Lord's Prayer, I join ranks with the disciples in the basic lessons of prayer—to sit, as they, upon the shoulders of Jesus so that he can carry me into the life of which he spoke when he said, "I am come that they may have life and have it abundantly" (John 10:10).

Our Father in Heaven

My religion is summed up in the first two words of the Lord's Prayer (Oliver Wendell Holmes).

As C. S. Lewis says, "Most people don't want God to be a father, who at times must be firm and tough as he raises his children. Most people want God to be a grandfather who, with 'senile benevolence,' just wants everyone to have a good time, no matter what the price, no matter what must be overlooked" (Duane Kelderman in *The Gentle Whisper*, page 56).

In his book, God and Man, Edward Schillibeecx focuses on the findings of child psychologists to make strikingly obvious what is obviously striking. The American child begins to speak at the age of eighteen months. Invariably, the first word formulated is "Da da, dad, daddy." At the same age level, a Jewish child in first-century Palestine would say in Aramaic, "Ab, Ab, Abba, Abba." The revolutionary revelation of Jesus lies precisely in this: the infinitely holy God in whose presence Moses had to remove his shoes, the God from whose fingertips universes fall, the God beside whose beauty the Grand Canyon is only a shadow, the God beside whose power the nuclear bomb is nothing, may be addressed with the same intimacy, familiarity, tenderness and reverence as an eighteen-month-old child resting on his father's lap (Brennan Manning in *Reflections for Ragamuffins*, p. 300).

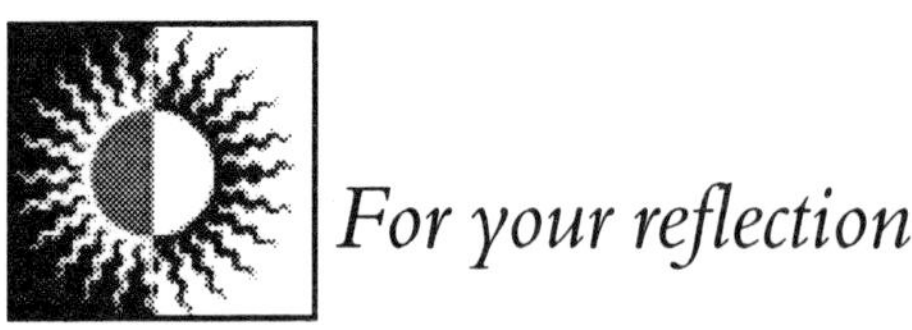

For your reflection

Our Most Wonderful Privilege

The Lord's Prayer is a key part of our corporate worship. We rarely gather together in worship without praying it. In every one of the special services of the church this prayer appears. In the service of Holy Communion it is our table prayer.

The Lord's Prayer is a part of our group devotionals. It is the moment in which we can unite together and know our identity together.

The Lord's Prayer is a part of our family devotions. In praying the Lord's Prayer all as a family are participating and involved.

The Lord's Prayer is also a part of our private, personal devotion. As we pray the prayer, we focus on God and we are inclusive in our intercessions. Furthermore, we are seeking from God that which links him to the totality of who we are and seek to be.

The Lord's Prayer is at the heart of our faith and worship. It is amazing in both its scope and content.

According to the Gospel of Luke, the disciples asked, "Lord, teach us to pray, as John taught his disciples." Jesus replied to the request by giving a prayer. "Pray these words," he says. This is the model for all praying. We will not get any further in our prayer lives than the progress we make in praying the Lord's Prayer.

The brevity of the Lord's Prayer is surprising. In less than 70 words, he gives us the "know how." We are a people today who abbreviate. We have a short attention span. This was not true in the day of our Lord. People were not hurried in their gatherings and in their prayers. Religious people prayed much and long. Jesus, however, in the midst of this setting, gives a short prayer.

There is more than brevity in the prayer. There is depth and inclusiveness. Dr. Gore has said that "it is not an exaggeration to say that the climax of Christian growth is to have thoroughly learned to say the Lord's Prayer in the spirit of him who first spoke it." Let someone ask you what your faith is. Respond with the Lord's Prayer, and you have shared your faith with that individual.

It is this amazing, loved prayer which has been called the greatest of all martyrs. In our praying of the Lord's Prayer we are often inattentive and our mind has a tendency to wander. The prayer is so familiar. It may be committed to memory quickly. We assume that we understand it. However, though a child can understand it, the wisest cannot exhaust it. This is a lifetime prayer involving a lifetime growth. Our familiarity tends to stunt our growth. A devout deacon chided his neighbor about his swearing. The reply came, "O well, Deacon, you know how it is. You pray a good deal and I swear a good deal, but neither of us means much by it."

Lest we be caught in meaningless prayer, I propose that we give personal attention to our praying of the Lord's Prayer. Often it is said, "Let us say the Lord's Prayer." Saying the prayer is not enough. Praying the prayer is what is needed. The heart and mind need to be involved in the speaking of the words.

Prayer is the communion of our hearts with God. In the communion of two persons there is togetherness and close relationship. In prayer there is togetherness with God. In prayer we really are exploring our relationship to God. In prayer we understand what God wants and why. In prayer we see the potentials of our life. In prayer we find ourselves more ready to let God lead us into the fulfillment of those potentials. The only reason we feel we have no time for prayer is that our life has been pulled apart and is disintegrating. Feeling we have no time is the greatest indication that we need to *take* time so that God can orient and pull us together again. There must be disciplined times for prayer. Spasmodic prayer is not enough; it tends to become selfish prayer. We call on God when we need help. Disciplined prayer is the exploration of life with God. Disciplined prayer shows we care. Al Ghazzali, the Moslem mystic, writes: "If you are never alone with God, it is not because you are too busy; it is because you don't care for him, don't like him. And you had better face the facts."

Our Father in Heaven

In this introductory to the prayer three words stand out and three facts are evident. The three words are *our, Father, heaven.* The three facts are unity, cheerfulness, confidence.

Our. As a youngster I wondered why in the Lord's Prayer I said "our Father" when I alone was praying. No longer do I wonder about this, for as a Christian I am always identified with the family of God, and as a person I am ever to be conscious of others. My prayer life would be suffocated if there were not a consciousness of others in my private moments with God. No individual can really say "my Father" who does not know God as "our Father."

The Old Testament is a book about God and his chosen people. The New Testament is a book about God and his chosen people, the new Israel, the Christian Church. The Bible is about God and the people of God. It is not God and *I.* It is God and *we.* The opening word of the Lord's Prayer is "our." We mean something to each other. The more isolated an individual is, the more destructive is the power of sin. The more deeply one becomes involved in the sin, the more disastrous is one's isolation.

Helpful is the reminder of the individual who wrote:

You cannot pray the Lord's Prayer
　　And even once say "I";
You cannot pray the Lord's Prayer
　　And even once say "my";
Nor can you pray the Lord's Prayer
　　And not pray for one another!
For when you ask for daily bread,
　　You must include your brother.
For others are included
　　In each and every plea;
From beginning to the end of it,
　　It does not once say "me."

Father. The idea of God as Father was not new with Jesus. He simply gave it strong emphasis. Some like to speak of God as the "Man Upstairs." Others want to think of God as the "Great Designer," the "Supreme Architect of the Universe," the "Oversoul," the "Unknowable One," the "Potentate," and the "Ruler of the Hearts and Reins of Men." How impersonal and limited are all these when contrasted with the terminology of Jesus—"Father." A good parent is one who protects and loves, one who plans and counsels, one who protects and provides. We think of a father as strong, dependable, creative, exemplary, loving, and even stern. God is our Father. By knowing him as our Father we know him as "thou" or "you," not "it." We also know we are neither displaced persons nor disinherited. We are God's children.

> But you have received a spirit of adoption. When we cry, "Abba! Father!" it is that very Spirit bearing witness with our spirit that we are children of God, and if children, then heirs, heirs of God and joint heirs with Christ—if, in fact, we suffer with him so that we may also be glorified with him (Romans 8:15b-17).

In Heaven. We are not taught to say "in heaven" so that we localize God. "Our Father in heaven" opens us to power and holiness. Heaven opens us to the fullness of God, to the awesome, to the awareness that God "is able to accomplish abundantly far more than all we can ask or imagine" (Ephesians 3:20).

Maybe you have had an experience of heaven in your life. A mother did. She had a son who was having problems in school. She thought he was being unfairly and unjustly treated. Her first impulse was to involve herself. On second thought, she decided to let the son work it out for himself. Then, as a parent is apt to do, she had other second thoughts. She worried. She was haunted by her son's problem. Finally one day, in a desperate attempt to find some peace of mind, she got in her car and drove out into the country. Pulling the car to the side of the road, she put her head on the steering wheel and began to cry. She cried and cried. Finally, when all cried out, she lifted her head and looked out at a great, golden field of wheat. She hadn't even noticed it when she stopped the car. Now it was there waving and dancing in the wind, and she was awake to it. She said, "I knew God was saying something to me in that wheat field. And so I dried my eyes, and I let its glories pour into me. I began to experience God's love. God did not send me an easy solution to my problem—just the assurance of his knowing and caring. And that was enough, because I knew that the same Fatherly love would reach down to touch my hurting child." For that mother heaven was now in her thinking and her living.

No wonder Martin Luther looked at those introductory words to the Lord's Prayer and in his Small Catechism declared:

> Here God encourages us to believe that he is truly our Father and we are his children. We therefore are to pray to him with complete confidence just as children speak to their loving father.

For Your Devotions

OUR Father in heaven

1 John 4: 13-21

Hymn: "Blest Be the Tie that Binds"

Lord God, the first word in the prayer your Son taught his disciples to pray is "our." As I come to you now, that word is on my lips and in my heart. At this point I come to you alone. Though I am alone in coming, I am really not alone, for in my aloneness your Son caused me to think of others. Often as I have prayed this prayer, I have prayed it with my family. Even now as I pray, they are with me. In almost every service of worship in my church I have prayed this prayer. Even now as I pray, the church family also is with me. In times of crisis and grief, it has been this prayer I have prayed. In meeting you, O God, I do so with the support of others who are praying too. What a strong reason for a sense of unity! What a reason also, O God, for gratitude! Thank you for taking me out of isolation and putting me in the company of the people of faith.

"Our"—it's such a little word and yet so big and mighty. It reminds me of the links with one another in the chain of love. It takes me more deeply into relationship with you, O God, for surely if I am to know and serve you whom I cannot see, then I must care and feel for your created people whom I do see. I am feeling, O Lord, a love for you and for others as the busyness of my life is interupted by this time of prayer with you.

Thus, Lord, I thank you for broadening my life. Thank you for teaching me to include those around me as I pray, for they are important if my life is to have wholeness and soundness. Thank you for enabling me to come to you in company with others. Thank you for welcoming everyone on equal footing and blotting out the differences I keep erecting. Thank you for curbing my selfishness. Thank you for brotherhood and sisterhood in life. Thank you for making humanity a family of faith.

Lord, in the happenings of life, may the constant be "our Father." Brace me with the conviction of the need for sacredness of expressions, lest I be profane in the claims I make and the ways in which I refer to you. Spare me from selfish possessiveness of you or from cutting out others by assuming you belong to me alone. Keep the initial thought and prayer of my life "our Father." Amen.

Our FATHER in heaven

Luke 15:11-32

Hebrew 12:5b-11

Hymns: "Father Eternal, Ruler of Creation"
"Great Is Thy Faithfulness"

Lord God, your Son, when he prayed, addressed you as Father. When his disciples asked him to teach them to pray, he told them to say, "Our Father." As I come to you saying, "Father," I am with Jesus in praying and saying, "Our Father." I also am with your people everywhere addressing you as "our Father." What a privilege to name you as Father, and to know you in this personal way.

Living as I do in a time when prejudice is rightly under attack and when sexism is rightly identified as evil, I am at times a bit uneasy and uncomfortable in saying, "Father." O Lord, spare me any sexism in addressing you as Father. Rather let me know you in a personal and loving relationship—as one who cares for me and who attends to the needs that arise. Help me to know my life as a gift from you, and that I can count on you just as a child counts on his or her parents. Joining with Jesus in the cry to you, O God, as Father, help me to treasure the identity of myself as your child. Joining in the cry to you, O God, as Father, enables me to feel at home with you and to anticipate the place which Jesus prepares for me.

There are those, O God, who have had rascals as fathers or who have known no worthy father. Calling you "Father" may not be pleasant or comforting for them as they remember their earthly father. May they in saying, "Our Father," be led to your love, your strength, and your promises for them.

As I think of you, O God, as Father, I am reminded how close you are, how accessible. My life is your idea and your creation. You were involved in my birth. You brought me into existence. You sustain me. As a good father you also discipline me. Spare me the evil of rejecting your firmness and the toughness of your love. Make sure that I do not look upon you as a mere gentle grandfather. Instead, keep my focus upon you as the responsible one upon whom I can rely and whose every care is for my growth in righteousness.

O God, Father of us all, thank you for inviting me through Christ to know you and pray to you as "our Father." Thanks for being as available to me as a parent. Amen.

Our Father IN HEAVEN

Revelation 21:1-7, 9-27

Hymns: "In Heaven Above, in Heaven Above"
"Surely Goodness and Mercy"

Naming you, O God, as "Father," I find myself in a bit of a quandary as I add the words "in heaven." Heaven is a mystery to me. I know it is your dwelling place. I know it also as a place that does not limit you. You are in heaven, yet you are here on earth. Heaven, Father, is also perfection to me. I have such piecemeal thought of what perfection is really like. Heaven is "up there" in my thought. "Up there" suggests freedom and release, whereas "down here" suggests being ground into the terrain, limited, even put to death. Heaven is eternal, beyond all creation, and somehow, O God, that is beyond anything I can imagine or think. The mention of heaven fills me with wonderment, awe, power, beauty, grandeur, rightness, and, not least, O God, your hiddenness.

I name you, O God, as "Father in heaven." You are beyond all creation. I am a creature of your creation. You are known, yet not known. You are imminent, yet transcendent. You are a paradox to me. Even that, O God, is beautiful. If you were fully comprehended, then life would be limited and confined for me. It is in the mystery of you, O God, I rest. As our "Father in Heaven," you are able to accomplish abundantly far more than all I can ask or imagine.

Bless the Lord, O my soul.
O Lord, my God, You are very great (Psalm 104:1).
Amen.

Hallowed Be Your Name

A literal translation of this first petition in the Norwegian reads: "Your name stands holy."

Luther said of this petition: "Among the seven petitions there is none greater for us to pray than, 'Hallowed be thy name.' . . . In this petition, God becomes everything and man becomes nothing."

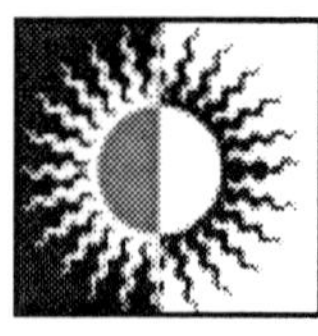

For your reflection:

Conquered by a Name

Do you think that God has his priorities mixed up? When he gave ten simple statements to Moses as an eye-opener to the understanding of life and a guide to living, one of the ten relates to his name. Years later when Jesus Christ provided his disciples with a short seven-petition prayer to teach them how to pray, one of the seven was a petition regarding the Lord's name. Is this emphasis upon the careful, cautious consideration and usage of the Lord's name that important? Does it really make that much difference what we do with the Lord's name and how we think about it?

Apparently people think not. Listen to the conversation of people and note the prominence of the Lord's name in that conversation. How glib and even careless much of that usage is. How profane!

Why all this fuss about a name? Why is the misuse so evil and the right use so important? Why do we usually end our prayers, "in the name of Jesus"?

As you seek answers to those questions and tune your life to the first petition of the Lord's Prayer, you might take a look at your own name and what that name means to you.

The first obvious fact is that your name identifies you. Your name admits you places. Your name brings things to you. Imagine a postal system without names. Your name designates you as a person. It keeps you from anonymity. Through it you gain credit. Through it you can also be discredited. Your name links you with your family. Your name may say other things about you too—for example it may suggest your nationality, religion, culture.

In fact, your name is interlinked with you to the extent that, when others hear your name, they immediately think of you. You and your name are one. Your name says something about your past. Your name speaks something of the present. Your name is that in your life which is observed by others. If yours is a good name, you have impressed people as a good person. If yours is a bad name, you have impressed them as bad. Your name makes for ease or difficulty. Your influence is largely dependent upon your name. What is true of your name is also true of others'. Some individuals have an easy life because they have established a good name for themselves. Others live complicated lives because of what has been linked with their name.

If you have been involved in arranging an event to which you want to draw a large crowd, you have been conscious of the power of a name to attract attention and attendance. You can plan an activity and have a speaker with a little-known name who has something wonderful, fresh, and vital to share, but draw a mediocre crowd. On the other hand, you can plan a program with a well-known speaker whose material is mediocre and have a large crowd. We can be beguiled by a name or led by a name.

Back in 1960, Elvis Presley, fresh out of Army khaki, appeared on an evening television program. For this he received $125,000. "He did two wiggles and sang two songs and for this received more than the yearly salary of the President of the United States and three times the yearly salary of the Chief Justice of the Supreme Court. An identical sum of money would pay the salaries of 25 school teachers, 42 ministers, or 63 farmhands in many of our states. It would provide a year's training for 30 or more nurses, would give 125 American young people a year in college, would stock 10 mission hospitals with elemental tools and drugs, would feed 3000 refugee children for a whole year" (*Christian Century*, May 25, 1960).

Now more than 30 years later, with Elvis dead more than half that time, there is still a mystique and fascination with the name Elvis Presley. We seem as a people to have problems finding an equilibrium in our estimates of economic worth because we are so attracted to names and are willing to pay exorbitantly to hear and see someone with a well-known name.

Why does God place such a premium upon his name that he dedicates one of ten commandments to the use of that name? Why does Jesus, in teaching us to pray, suggest that when we pray, we say, "Hallowed be your name"? When you ponder the significance of your own name, the answer becomes obvious. When you ponder the names of people and the power of names upon your life, then the power and the impact of God's name is no longer a mystery.

Our Lord is jealous of his name precisely because what he means and can do for us is dependent upon his name and the relationship of that name to us. If the forces of evil can destroy the worth of his name, they have destroyed the power of God in human lives. To swear or curse is to pray negatively. It is not robbing God of his power, it is simply isolating the power of God. No one can know the power of God without knowing the name of God as a holy name. In a real sense, what we do with God's name is what we do with God.

This is illustrated in a little story concerning the American storywriter, O. Henry. The real name of O. Henry was Sydney Porter. As a young man this Texan was imprisoned for embezzlement. While imprisoned he met a guard named Oren Henry. When it came time to leave prison instead of carrying out his old, disgraced name, he decided to take the name of his guard, O. Henry. The story is told that, as he went through the prison doors, the old guard said to him, "Take good care of our name." The comment of that guard was much more than a reference to a name. It involved the whole person leaving prison that day. Likewise, when we pray, "Hallowed be your name," we are not only referring to a title we give our Lord; we are saying something about our whole relationship to the Lord. That relationship is strong and kept intact as we hallow that which is our primary and outward identity with God, that is his name.

In the last century the German biologist Haeckel repudiated the idea of a creator. He insisted that a primal substance, which he called "mobile cosmic ether," was the cause of the universe. Imagine praying, "O Mobile Cosmic Ether, hallowed be your name." If this were true, we would not pray. We pray because the God we know in Christ is our Father who cares for us. His name is to be a hallowed name, for within the orbit of his interest, concern and love he includes us. We are praying in the first petition not for the hallowing of a substance but for the hallowing of him who hallows us.

The word "hallowed" is rooted in the word "holy." Years ago Harold K. Schilling, dean of the graduate school of Pennsylvania State University and professor of physics, was reading Dr. Abraham Joshua Herschel's *Man's Quest for God*. He noted that the Jewish rabbi was insisting that God's demand upon us is that we are to be more than good. We are to be holy. Dr. Schilling said that he had assumed that holy really referred to being good. However, he probed the word and discovered that religion is not primarily a matter of the emotions. Nor is religion primarily concerned with ethics or morals. Indeed the religious life must include these. But the religious life is much more. The word which expresses this is the word "holy." The Christian life is richer and more meaningful than the good life. It is life lived in the conscious presence of God. It is life lived not only in the physical dimension, but also in the spiritual. It's the "liberated life, the life of the uninhibited soaring mind, the life not chained to the physical or even to the aesthetic. . . . The holy life is then a life above and beyond the good life, because, though it certainly must have the dimension of goodness, it has also that dimension which gives it extension in the realm of the divine."

When we pray, "hallowed be your name," we are thus seeking a life lived in the presence of the Lord. We are seeking a holy faith and holy living. The further we are from God, the easier it is to profane the name of God. The closer we are to God, the more likely we are to hallow his name. As Sri Ramakrishna noted, "If a man repeats God's name, his body, mind, and everything becomes pure."

This first petition is not only a matter of God's identity, it is also a matter of our personal identity. We are in God's family. We bear God's name. What we do with God's name we are doing with our own identity.

This first petition is linked also to the conclusion of the Lord's Prayer, the doxology of praise. Life is hallowed by the exalted purposes and motivation of God. Life is to be lived with more than a sense of goodness. Life is to be lived with God. To hallow God's name is to know what Peter means when he writes:

> But you are a chosen race, a royal priesthood, a holy nation, God's own people, in order that you may proclaim the mighty acts of him who called you out of darkness into his marvelous light. Once you were not a people, but now you are God's people; once you had not received mercy, but now you have received mercy (1 Peter 2:9-10).

For Your Devotions

HALLOWED BE Your Name

Isaiah 6:1-5

Hymn: "Holy, Holy, Holy"

Lord, as the words of your Son, "hallowed be your name," roll across my lips, I am reminded of the passage in Isaiah where the seraphs carrying you upon a throne are calling to one another,

> Holy, holy, holy is the Lord of hosts;
> The whole earth is full of his glory.

Life and things can become so mundane and ordinary, but you are distinctive and special, O Lord. You are holy. You would have us live with a sense of the extraordinary. Wherever I turn, whatever I do, help me, O Lord, to pray, "Hallowed be." Keep me from making life cheap and tawdry. Through knowledge of the holy, harness me to that which is worthy and glorious. Keep me from complaint and link me to the noble challenges of life so that, like Paul, I "press on toward the prize of the high calling." Spare me the pessimism of earthly limitations, and release me for the optimism of life in which I can rejoice in being "more than conqueror." Give me, I pray, "the idea of the holy" and help me to carry it forth in all that I am.

Lord, teaching me to pray, "Hallowed be your name," you take me into the courts of heaven. It is on a high and lofty plane that I meet you. Before I really seek anything from you, I am exalting and praising.

"Hallowed be your name." As these four words roll across my lips, I find myself thinking: am I in petition or am I expressing an affirmation? My prayer life, O Lord, rests upon affirmation. All that I am and seek in prayer rests upon the affirmation I make about you. Without affirmation all is a void, and I am in a state of nothingness. With affirmation all is a positive stance and a joyous anticipation. O Lord, I would affirm your holiness, your otherness. You are a credit to this world, to all life. With you there are no regrets.

Even as I affirm I am also, O Lord, in petition, for I need to know more of your holiness. I need to hallow more than I now hallow. I come seeking to exalt and glorify you. I come desiring to fall into step with you. I come hoping to unify my adoration with the here and now. Amen.

Hallowed be YOUR NAME

John 17:25-26

Hymn: "How Sweet the Name of Jesus Sounds"

Lord, I am struck by the fact that out of seven prayer petitions, one relates to your name. I am also struck by the fact that out of ten commandments governing human action, one relates solely to the usage of your name. "Hallowed be your name."

Lord, when I'm tempted to make light of your name, remind me how important my own name is to me. It is my identity. It carries my reputation. My name and I walk through life together. Destroy my name, and I'm destroyed. My name and I are one. Your name and you, O Lord, are one. Your name is more than a symbol. It is you. What you mean to me is largely what your name means to me. If you are to be a refuge and strength for me, then your name must be that high and lofty name in which the recall brings solace and power. If in you is my salvation, then your name must be for me a saving name rather than a cursing acclamation. In your name, Lord, is everything you are to me. It is as I repeat your name that my body, mind, and spirit become pure and holy.

O Lord, frequent are the glib usages of Your name. Vicious are the ways in which your name is profaned. Thoughtless are the ways in which it is involved in our conversations. "Hallowed be your name," O Lord. Paying attention to your name is paying attention to the roots of my life. May I take your name seriously so that I take you seriously. Make sure that I rightly reverence your name so that I may rightly know the pathway I shall follow. Remind me that in your name is my name for, as a baptized child of yours, I own your holy, precious name. Let me never forget that what I ask in your name you have promised you will do. As your name crosses my lips, may it always be a name that goes forth to accomplish your saving mission in the lives of all who inhabit your creation. Give me the grit to be faithful that I may have the grace to be fruitful. All this, O Lord, I ask in your name. Amen.

Your Kingdom Come

A little girl was saying her bedtime prayers and, for the first time, was trying to get through the Lord's Prayer on her own. She started off beautifully: "Our Father, who art in heaven, hallowed be thy name." Then she became a little confused: "Thy kingdom come, thy kingdom go. . . ." A confused child, but good theology. That kingdom for which we pray every Sunday, that kingdom governed by the rule of God, that divine/human realm of delicate truths, that kingdom of right relationships comes to us as God's pure gift and goes with us as our pure gift to others. The kingdom of God is developing within our own lives. Each of us is being offered the power to make God's kingdom more and more visible on earth. Each of us is being offered the power to proclaim God's kingdom of love (*Sunday Sermons*, Voicing Publications, October 2, 1988).

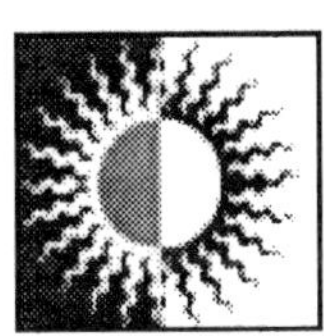

For your reflection

Expecting an Invasion

Is the second petition of the Lord's Prayer, "Your kingdom come," outdated? For centuries kings and queens were the glue that held a nation together. That is no longer true. Now royalty is pomp and ceremony with little power and authority. When we today pray, "Your kingdom come," we may be hard pressed to know for what we are praying.

There are no less than 162 references in the New Testament to the kingdom of God. The idea of a baby born in Bethlehem as a king got Herod uptight and caused him to order the slaughter of the baby boys of the city. The possibility that Jesus might be a king put Pontius Pilate in a difficult role on the initial Good Friday. A wish to see Jesus as king may have prompted Judas Iscariot to betray Jesus.

The petition, "Your kingdom come," was a troublesome concept in Jesus' day. It is still a troublesome concept.

In the *Small Catechism* Martin Luther raised the question, "What does this [this praying of 'your kingdom come'] mean?" His answer:

> God's kingdom comes indeed
> without our praying for it,
> but we ask in this prayer that it
> may come also to us.

Luther is suggesting that our prayer does not determine whether or not God's kingdom comes. Like the dawn in the morning it comes whether we pray or not. The question is really whether or not this coming will include us. Luther went on in the *Small Catechism* to say:

> God's kingdom comes when our heavenly Father gives us
> his Holy Spirit, so that by his grace we believe his holy word
> and live a godly life on earth now and in heaven forever.

When you pray, "Your kingdom come," you are really saying, "God, I know your kingdom is coming. As it comes, I want to be a part of it. When it comes, don't leave me out."

When you pray, "Your kingdom come," you are praying for faith. God and his kingdom mean little to you unless there is faith.

To pray, "Your kingdom come," is to reach out for the unlimitedness of God. We human beings are a restless people whose restlessness is satisfied only in God. There is within each of us a resistance to the King and his kingdom. We tend to take it only in part. We seem unwilling to trust. We forget that we belong to the King. We forget from whom we come and to whom we belong. We split life as if we belonged to many dominions. This tension within us blinds us to the greatness, the grace, the glory of the kingdom of our God. In this petition we pray that we might be people of a single heart. We pray that the King might fully conquer our hearts and that we might know the full joy of his kingdom.

The kingdom of God is the kingdom of forgiveness and grace. This is the kingdom in which we know that, though we are sinners, we can be reconciled. This is the kingdom where the chains of sin and the fear of judgment depart. This is the kingdom in which we know we are loved and where we love. God's kingdom is the rule of God in the hearts and lives of people because it first is the kingdom of grace. God's kingdom is the kingdom of glory because it first is the kingdom of grace. God is not a ruling despot or tyrant. God is the loving Father who as King treats us as children.

To pray, "Your kingdom come," is not only to seek answers to our own personal needs. It is also an intercession for others. This petition is a great prayer for missions as it sends us forth as missionaries in the world. To pray this petition is to seek sensitivity to the needs around us. In contemplation of the kingdom we are aroused to the actions of the kingdom.

If you visit with people in business, you may hear them talking of how tough the business world is today. Chat with laborers, and you may hear them speak of how laboring people must look after themselves, because management takes unfair advantage. Speak to pastors, and they may tell how difficult work in their parish can be. Meet church members, and they may complain of the unreasonable demands of their pastors. Converse with parents, and they may tell of how uncooperative their children are. So often in our society, we seem to meet self-pity. So many people seem to think life is a raw deal, and he or she has received the worst deal of all. People appear to be building their own little kingdoms, looking after their own little bailiwicks. Now turn to the pages of Scripture and read the story of Christ. There is no self-pity here. He came to establish the kingdom of his Father. This Father is our Father too. As we pray, "Your kingdom come," we are praying a change in our lives from self-pity and self-service to kingdom concern and kingdom service. We are seeking to be bearers of the cross.

Readied for change does not mean we are to look for a new place or a new assignment. Rather, it means we anticipate a new inner spirit. No longer are we to do what we do with an eye for what we can get for ourselves. Now the big word of our lives is the word "give"—what can I give to alleviate and lessen the misery of life for others? Now I am released from giving complaint to giving compliments. Now I am willing to go the second mile.

An anonymous writer explored what it means to be in God's kingdom (*Faith At Work*, March 1976):

> After my prayer list became unwieldly, I decided that instead of a lengthy prayer for each person, I would picture each person in my mind and ask God to bless that person that day. In following this plan, I learned something about myself. I discovered that for several persons—especially members of my own family—it was difficult to simply say, "Lord, bless this person today." For example, I had been praying that the Lord would help my son, Billy, to be more organized, praying that God would make Billy like I wanted him to be! I choked on the prayer, "Lord, bless Billy today," because that meant I had to accept him just as he was—messy, unorganized, etc. As I prayed a prayer of blessing for Billy, I found that it became easier to accept him as he was. The same thing happened with other members of my family and friends. Pretty soon my prayer evolved to, "Lord make me a blessing to Billy." And I started thinking, "How can I be a blessing to my family today?" Now what I'm working on is finding out God's prayer for a person, God's wants for that person, and pray that prayer instead of one I think is appropriate.

The kingdom of God "is not food and drink," says Paul. It is "righteousness and peace and joy in the Holy Spirit" (Romans 14:17). "The kingdom of God depends not on talk but on power" (1 Corinthians 4:20). The kingdom of God, Jesus said, belongs to "the poor in spirit," to those "persecuted for righteousness' sake" (Matthew 5:3, 10), and to those who do "the will of [the] Father in heaven" (Matthew 7:21). Jesus also said, "Let the little children come to me, and do not stop them; for it is to such as these that the kingdom of heaven belongs" (Matthew 19:14).

The kingdom of God is "like a grain of mustard seed" (Matthew 13:31), "like yeast" (Matthew 13:33), "like treasure hidden in a field"

(Matthew 13:44), "like a merchant in search of fine pearls" (Matthew 13:45), "like a net that was thrown into the sea and caught fish of every kind" (Matthew 13:47), and "like a landowner who went out early in the morning to hire laborers for his vineyard" (Matthew 20:1). The kingdom of God "may be compared to someone who sowed good seed in his field" (Matthew 13:24), "to a king who gave a marriage banquet for his son" (Matthew 22:2), and to ten bridesmaids who "took their lamps and went to meet the bridegroom" (Matthew 25:1).

> Once Jesus was asked by the Pharisees when the kingdom of God was coming, and he answered, "The kingdom of God is not coming with things that can be observed; nor will they say, 'Look, here it is!' or 'There it is!' For, in fact, the kingdom of God is among you" (Luke 17:20-21).

In the words of Daniel Ch. Overduin, "In Bethlehem we see its appearance. In Gethsemane and at Calvary we see its price. In Joseph's garden and on the Mount of Ascension we see its victory. At present we see its glorious future."

"Kingdom" has been called "the most important word in the vocabulary of our Lord." It marks that point wherever God is in charge. For us to pray "Your kingdom come" is to invite God to bring about God's complete and ultimate rule. It is to seek an invasion, the full and final takeover of the Lord.

For your devotions:

YOUR KINGDOM come

Romans 14:17

Hymns: "Your Kingdom Come! O Father, Hear Our Prayer"
"Oh, Worship the King"

I have come to you as Father. I come to you now as King. Lord, I ask for your kingdom to come. Living in democratic America, I find thought of a kingdom remote. I do understand, however, that it involves royalty, citizenship, and authority. To be in a kingdom gives root, identity, and responsibility, as well as privilege. All this you have promised to me in the birth of water and the Spirit.

Lord, I would contemplate your kingdom. I would pray that it might not be remote, but that it would be a factor in my everyday thought and encounter. I would be resigned to its authority. I would have its righteousness, peace, and joy permeate every recess and corner of my being. Fill me with love for your kingdom and you as king. Be the leaven, the treasure, the pearl of my life.

O Lord, to be child of a king! I can scarcely comprehend what it all means. The apostle Peter said, "But you are a chosen race, a royal priesthood, a holy nation, God's own people, in order that you may proclaim the mighty acts of him who called you out of darkness into his marvelous light" (1 Peter 2:9). Lord, help me to believe that. Your Son said, "The kingdom of God is not coming with things that can be observed; nor will they say, 'Look, here it is!' or 'There it is!' For, in fact, the kingdom of God is among you" (Luke 17:20-21). Lord, help me in faith to discern that.

Some would suggest that life is a raw deal and a sick joke, even a dirty trick. But you, O Lord, have taught me to pray, "Your kingdom come," so that I might know life is precious, awesome, and always hopeful. You have taught me to pray, "Your kingdom come," so that I might live well. "My God, how wonderful thou art, thy majesty how bright! How beautiful thy mercy seat. . . ." I know your kingdom is your rule. I know it bespeaks authority. But, Lord, I know it is first and foremost forgiveness and grace. Before your throne I would prostrate myself, O King. Amen.

Your kingdom COME

Mark 4:30-32

Hymns: "Your Kingdom Come, O Father"
"Lift Up Your Heads, Ye Mighty Gates"

Lord, your kingdom has come. It came when you made a covenant with Abraham. It came when your son was born of Mary. It came to me when I was baptized. Today I herald you as king of my life. I believe that your kingdom has come to me. I rejoice that your Holy Spirit has called me through the gospel, enlightened and enlisted me to faith. I am pleased to know that my citizenship is in heaven.

Lord Jesus Christ, your kingdom is coming. Confident as I am of the presence of your kingdom, I still pray, "Your kingdom come." I hail the continuous coming of your kingdom. There is much of Your kingdom which needs to be the kingdom for me. There is much of your kingship that needs to be authoritative for me. Righteousness, peace, and joy have only skimmed the surface of my life. I pray that they may permeate the whole of what I am and do.

Lord Jesus Christ, your kingdom will come. As I think of your kingdom, Lord, I think of the great beyond to which death is the transition point. I am a pilgrim here, and heaven is my home. "I go to heaven wherever I go." Heaven comes, and its coming needs be the mainstay of my life. May this glorious hope make me "steadfast, immovable, always excelling" in your work, O Lord.

I come to you with an invitation: "Come! Come and take charge!" You alone are competent. You alone are reliable. You alone understand how the past, present, and future interlink. Come and be my King. Come and let your kingdom be my commonwealth. To you may I look for the guidance, the direction, the empowerment, and the security. Upon you alone may I rely. Help me to seek first your kingdom and your righteousness, trusting you to provide all else of which I have need. So be it, Lord! So be it! Amen.

Your Will Be Done, on Earth as It Is in Heaven

This petition has been called "the central petition" of the prayer. It has also been called our noblest expression to God. If ever an individual rises to full stature, if an individual is ever all that God intends, it is at this point when he or she can say to God, "I trust you. Let your will be done."

> He who wills to believe shall never lack reasons for believing (C. H. Spurgeon).

> Take my will and make it thine;
> It shall be no longer mine (Frances B. Havergal).

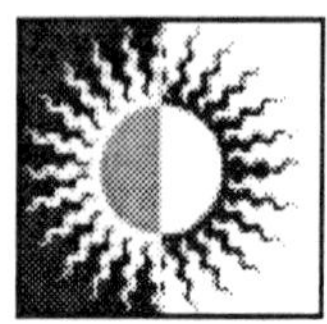

For your reflection:

Our Noblest Expression to God

You have a will. It is one of the greatest gifts you have in life. Your will designates your inclination, your desire, your choice, your passion, your determination. When someone says to you, "I will," you can count on it happening, for it means a decision has been reached. When you on your wedding day answered the pastor's question, "I will," it meant that you had made a lifelong commitment to your spouse. Never again would you look for someone to be your spouse. That decision had been concluded. To your spouse you were now committed.

"I will" is not only a decision. It is also the energy to back up that decision. This is manifest in "the will to live" and the way it prolongs life. I remember a Minneapolis man who, based on every health and physical indication, should have died six months before he did. One factor made the difference. He willed to see his son one time more. He had to wait six months for his son stationed in Europe to obtain a leave and to return home.

Your will, my will is a great gift. But it can be triggered by the wrong center. It can put us in conflict with each other, with God, and even with ourselves. Jesus understood that. In teaching us to pray, He asks us to pray, "Your will be done." Jesus calls us to have our will cleansed and re-directed by the Father's will. Jesus urges us to desire and to seek a resignation of our will to the higher will of God.

To pray, "Your will be done, on earth as in heaven," may completely change the way we view prayer. Prayer is no longer a technique for getting things. Consider these responses to prayer: A young adult set out on an extensive journey with a few pennies in her pocket. She was determined to prove to herself and to others that God answers prayer and he would provide for her needs.

The author of a sermon published by Voicing Publications shared a "thank you" letter which appeared in the newsletter of a popular radio and TV evangelist: "Please publish my thanks to the good Lord for many favors received, among them the obtaining of an auto driver's license for my nephew, who has very poor vision. His business was dependent on his ability to drive his car—(signed) Mrs. L.S., North Carolina." Beneath the letter appeared the editor's response: "Residents of North Carolina are warned to watch out for a devout nephew with thick eyeglasses. Residents of heaven are asked to stop kidding auto license inspectors."

The action of that young adult, as well as the letter to that television evangelist, suggest something of the dilemma in which we are placed when we view prayer as a technique for getting. Prayer then becomes a way of having my need answered at the expense of yours. Prayer becomes an attempt to procure a sensational action of God. Jesus refused his hometown folk at Nazareth when they sought to make him a sensationalist. He did the same when Herod the Tetrarch sought a miracle on Good Friday. Jesus, when tempted by Satan to be a sensationalist, responded, "You must not put the Lord your God to the test."

The third petition is not only the central petition of the Lord's Prayer, it is also the central factor of the whole experience of prayer.

It was Raymond Sheehan who noted:

> When the first Christians came to worship they had two parts to their service. The first part was for anyone who might wish to attend. The second section, however, was reserved only for the truly committed, the ones whose discipleship had been attested and certified. Significantly, it was during this latter part that the Lord's Prayer was used. Limited only to the assembly of true believers, the ancient Syrian Liturgy of Saint James had as its preface to the Lord's Prayer the following: "Count us worthy, O Lord, Lover of men, with confidence, with pure heart, with contrite soul, with face unashamed, with sanctified lips, to be bold to invoke Thee, the Holy God in Heaven, as our Father, and to say . . ."

In the third petition, we are in acquiescence to the will of God. In scores of languages "prayer" is translated simply "to speak with God." In one language (the Tzotzil), "prayer" is "asking with one's heart exposed." That definition seems more in tune with what Jesus taught, for in prayer we are exposed, we come out from under our self-protective covering. Prayer is not my will imposed upon God. It is my will in submission to God. It is my priorities seen in the context of God's will, rather than being born of my selfishness.

When we propose that prayer in the light of the third petition of the Lord's Prayer is acquiescence, it may not be particularly palatable. We tend more toward assertiveness than we do to acquiescence. We are a people seeking freedom, and to us acquiescence is akin to bondage rather than freedom. What seems difficult to understand is the fact that when we surrender our own will and accept God's will we are really free. It was when Adam and Eve exerted their own wills in opposition to the will of God that they lost their freedom and entered bondage. Christ, on the other hand, in the Garden of

Gethsemane was a fully liberated person. In his Gethsemane prayer, "Nevertheless, not my will but thine be done," he was united with God the Father, and he moved in a oneness with the Father to fulfill his mission.

This earthly existence in which we live has been called an "eternal wrestling match." About us and even within us are the evil schemes and purposes of the devil, the world, and our own sinful self. We cry out, "Your kingdom come," and then we proceed to construct our own kingdom and to shout, "I am the king of the hill." We cry out, "Hallowed be your name," and then we act as if we are a people unsure of the holy. We profane and cheapen life. In this eternal wrestling match we are invited to pray, "Your will be done." We are then seeking for God and the good to prevail. We are seeking the defeat of evil. We are letting go and letting God.

When you pray, "Your will be done," Jesus adds "on earth as in heaven." He did not add those words to the first petition, "Hallowed be your name," or to the second, "Your kingdom come." But can we doubt that, though unspoken, they are part of those petitions too? In our wrestling match something is happening when we pray, "Your will be done, on earth as in heaven." It is not seeking mere pennies from heaven. It is not even asking God to prove himself. It is something deeper, more profound, more exciting. It's what novelist Anne Douglas Sedgwick witnessed when in a painful illness she wrote a friend:

> Now, added to everything else, I can't breathe unless lying down my ribs collapse. Yet, I can't drink my food sitting up. Life is a queer struggle. Yet it is mine and beautiful to me. There is joy in knowing I lie in the hands of God. When you wrote, "Your spirit can surmount anything," I felt a strange tremor of response from an indomitable thread of life within me. It is mine, but I feel it communicated from God.

Praying the third petition, we are open to a communication from God. Praying the third petition, we seek for God to prevail.

> "[God's] will is done when he strengthens our faith and keeps us firm in his Word as long as we live" (Martin Luther in the *Small Catechism*).

For your devotions

YOUR WILL be done, on earth as in heaven

Matthew 12:46-50

Hymns: "What God Ordains Is Always Good"
"Have Thine Own Way, Lord"

Lord, I am troubled. Your Son taught his disciples to pray, "Your will be done." Am I ready to pray, "Your will be done"? Dare I? This petition is the point of decision. To pray "Your will be done," suggests I am willing to let your will take precedence over my own. To pray, "your will be done," suggests I am ready to set aside the world and my own self-interests for you and your kingdom. To pray, "Your will be done," suggests I'm determined to be a Christian even if it runs contrary to what is espoused in the world.

Lord, I yearn to be big enough to pray, "Your will be done." As I have sought the coming of your kingdom, now I seek the doing of your will. Without taking hold of your will, the coming of your kingdom is but a fleeting fantasy, a passing whim. Only when your will is done does your kingdom come.

As your Son struggled in Gethsemane to be resigned to the will of the Father, so I too, Lord, struggle to be accepting of your will. Often my own selfishness looms large, and I would like to run its path. I seek to justify my will thinking acquiescence to you and others is a weakness. I let my desires be colored by the mandates of the world. I tire of conflict with evil. O Lord, help me to see the folly of my own will when it conflicts with your will. Instead of seeking to impress my will upon you and others, O Lord, bring me to a desire to have my will resigned to your will. Assist me to be a person big enough for repentance, honest enough for confession of sin and faith. Illumine my life with the clear direction and mandate of your will.

Make clear to me your will. Spare me the game of pretending your will cannot really be known. Is not your will, O Lord, to be found in anything that draws me together with others in love, service, and sacrifice? Is not your will, O Lord, that which keeps me accepting responsibilities rather than succumbing to license and excuse-making? Is not your will, O Lord, that which makes me so at home with the good that, before I even ask what is the good to be done, I am doing it?

Lord, I come in prayer asking you to temper my requests by enveloping them in the constancy of your will. Keep me aware of the importance of making the right decision. Safeguard me from making those decisions only with self in mind. Keep me mindful that what I choose for today affects what happens tomorrow.

Lord, you have shown that your will is also a will laced with grace and mercy. Help me not forget. Keep reminding me that your will is the door opening to life abundant and eternal. Amen.

Your will BE DONE, ON EARTH AS IN HEAVEN

Romans 12:1-2

Hymns: "Forth in Thy Name, O Lord, I Go"
"Only One Life"

Lord, as I voice, "Your will be done, on earth as in heaven," I am mindful of two gaps needing to be bridged. One is the gap between what I ought to be and what I am. What I ought to be is your will for my life. What I am falls short of your will. I pray you to convince me of the folly of sin. I pray you to convince me of the fullness of salvation. I pray you to convince me of your grace and your will which empower me for new beginnings. I pray you to convince me of your judgments as the right judgments, of your judgments as the way evil is stripped away. O Lord, bridge the gap between what I ought to be and what I am. Keep me moving across the bridge from the imperfections of my present life to the perfections inherent to do your will.

The second gap needing to be bridged, O Lord, is the gap between heaven and this earth. What a beauty there is in life when we human beings let the marks of heaven be the marks of life! What potentials there are for happiness and well-being. The world is filled with inequities, injustice, and wars. We human beings seem bent on self-destruction.

> I come seeking that this earth would know your will and
> have your will be done—
> Your will be done in the way we relate to and care for
> this earth.
> Your will be done in the way we relate to, feel for, and act
> for each other.
> Your will be done in the way we think about our own
> selves—body, mind, and spirit.
> Your will be done in our vocations, in our recreation and
> avocations, in our eating and our drinking.
> Your will be done when we're suffering and when in
> time of affluence all unfolds so well for us.

Lord, bridge that gap between heaven and earth, reminding us that you want our earthly lives to be lived in your presence. Spare us the pain which marks life alienated from your will. Remind me often, O Lord, that you really have two homes, "one in heaven, the other in the lowest heart." Amen.

Give Us Today Our Daily Bread

Jesus bids us to pray for bread. It is to be noted, however, that He does not wish us to pray for cake (Ernest Fremont Tittle).

Here we consider the poor bread-basket—the needs of our body and our life on earth. It is a brief and simple word but very comprehensive. When you pray for "daily bread" you pray for everything that is necessary in order to have and enjoy daily bread and, on the contrary, against everything that interferes with enjoying it. You must therefore enlarge and extend your thoughts to include not only the oven or the flour bin, but also the broad fields and the whole land which produce and provide for us our daily bread and all kinds of sustenance. For if God did not cause grain to grow and did not bless and preserve it in the field, we could never take a loaf of bread from the oven to set on the table.

To put it briefly, this petition includes everything that belongs to our entire life in this world; only for its sake do we need daily bread. . . .

But especially is this petition directed against our chief enemy, the devil, whose whole purpose and desire it is to take away or interfere with all we have received from God. He is not satisfied to obstruct and overthrow spiritual order, so that he may deceive men with his lies and bring them under his power, but he also prevents and hinders the establishment of any kind of government or honorable and peaceful relations on earth. This is why he causes so much contention, murder, sedition, and war, why he sends tempest and hail to destroy crops and cattle, why he poisons the air, etc. In short, it pains him that anyone receives a morsel of bread from God and eats it in peace. If it were in his power, and our prayer to God did not restrain him, surely we would not have a straw in the field, a penny in the house, or even our life for one hour—especially those of us who have the Word of God and would like to be Christians (Martin Luther in the *Large Catechism*).

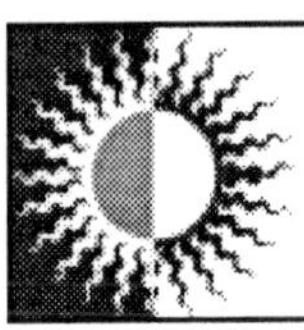

For your reflection

Eating from the Divine Pantry

In the opening petitions of the Lord's Prayer we embrace God. In the fourth petition we embrace the world. We move now to the pronouns "us" and "our." A Peanuts comic strip portrayed Snoopy the dog saying, "There's one thing I've always been proud of, and that's the fact that I'm independent." Charlie Brown appears with Snoopy's meal. Then Snoopy's thinking changes and he says, "Well, maybe I'm sort of semi-dependent."

In the fourth petition we are face-to-face with our dependence upon God. We are also face-to-face with our dependence upon each other. The fact is that God's bread comes to us "family style." It has been suggested that in praying the Lord's Prayer we are praying "give us day by day our daily discovery." That discovery is a discovery of God and, as for Snoopy, it is also a discovery of others.

The story is told of a little boy named Chris who ended his prayer: "And, please, Lord, put the vitamins in pie and cake instead of in cod liver oil and spinach. Amen." But that is not the way Jesus taught us to pray. Rather, Jesus taught us to pray for daily bread.

Daily bread is an inclusive word. It embraces all the necessities of life. Psychologists tell us there are six basic needs of human life: food and drink, sleep, communication, waking, cleanliness, and sexual satisfaction. "Whenever we find people, we find them building the hymns, the symphonies, the jazz, the folk-tunes, or the tom-tom rhythms of their lives out of these basic notes in the scale of human existence" (Wayne Oates). We concern ourselves with these needs when we pray the fourth petition. We face our needs with God.

"Give *us* . . . *our* daily bread." Notice the pronouns "us" and "our." When I eat my bread, I am to be mindful of bread belonging to another. Our Lord, both in this petition and in the seventh commandment, gives validity to private ownership. Our Lord, however, puts that ownership in the context of sensitivity to others. We might call it breaking bread with compassionate concern.

"Give . . . this day . . . daily bread." Need, our need is now. You cannot build a stockpile philosophy on the basis of the model prayer. Day by day we are to depend upon God to provide. We are not to let today become cluttered by the uncertainties of tomorrow. We are to be alive in every way today. Our ambition and effort is for today. If this provides for tomorrow, fine, but let your life be alive today. The Christian faith is an action faith rather than a procrastination. Christ did not wait for the next day to do the good which needed to be done today. You can expect God's best help today, for this is the day of his primary concern. Carry this confidence into every day, for this is the confidence with which he would have you pray.

The question might come to mind, "Why pray this petition?" God knows our needs. He provides. Why pray over such little and seemingly insignificant things as bread?

Basically, we must pray the fourth petition because God has invited us thus to pray; furthermore, we have great need to pray for our basic needs. Our physical needs, raw as they may at times seem, are a matter of such importance and concern that we cannot bear them alone. We must pray.

If we could not pray to God for the daily bread of life, how could we pray about anything? If God was not concerned with all our needs, we could not depend on God in any need. If God were not concerned about all needs, he would be divorced, out of touch, and impersonal. He would be a God who does not connect. Christianity has been called "the most material religion in the world." Christianity, as J.V.L. Casserley has said, "takes material reality seriously, loves it, respects it, sees the fundamental decency of the scientist's quest for knowledge about it and, more than that, realizes that . . . our task in the spiritual life is to make the material conditions of life reflect the spiritualities. . . . Spirit is defined by showing its power to mold matter to its purposes and make matter serve." In Christianity the body is not evil. It is the temple of the Holy Spirit. Canon Raven, in an hour of hideous despair, happened to see a drop of water gleaming in the dim light of a field lantern. In that drop of water he became conscious of God's faithfulness and care. It could not have happened if his faith had taught him to divorce God from daily bread.

God is the source. Life is hallowed in all areas. Physical life is not really something dirty and rotten. Money per se is not filthy lucre. God connects all the parts of our life.

> Back of the loaf is the snowy flour
> And back of the flour the mill,
> And back of the mill is the wheat and the shower,
> And the sun and the Father's will.
> (Babcock)

We know this. The fourth petition reveals to us that God's Spirit is at work in all the processes by which the bread is made. In this petition Christ hallows the daily work of our lives. Further, through this petition God makes us stewards. We are in vital touch with God who gives that we might use the gifts and properties of life in meaningful service. There is correlation between this petition and what we do with the offering plate on a Sunday morning. There is a correlation between this petition and our dinner table. There is a correlation between this petition and the work we do.

A further need for us to pray this petition is our need to be released from worry. A moment ago we mentioned six basic needs of life. It has been said there are six basic fears which accompany sleepless nights; they are criticism, sickness, poverty, lack of love, old age, and death. A steamship company ran a full-page advertisement in a magazine. The advertisement carried a picture of a beautiful ocean liner with the caption, "No finer food or service afloat or ashore." Above the picture were strung in large lettering the words, "A world away from worry on the world's fastest ship." The ad was a beautiful thing. The only trouble with it was its untruthfulness. The great bulwark against worry is not a trip on a ship. It is trust. Placing trust in a ship or in a house or in a fortune will let us down. In the fourth petition Christ encourages us to put our trust in God knowing that when we do there is hope, and our worries lose their grip upon us.

In praying this petition Jesus reminds us that we are benefactors. Like the one leper, rather than the nine, we return to give thanks. Two persons come to my mind. Both are confined to their homes. One is a miserable, unhappy person. The other is happy, cheerful, and pleasant. The difference between the two? The first lives forgetting to thank. The second person lives in thankfulness. Thankfulness turns us outward. In thankfulness we give. In thanklessness we are turned in upon ourselves. The fourth petition is not only a petition in which we ask. It also prompts thanksgiving.

Through praying this petition we learn to trust, we learn to thank, and we become aware of our stewardship. Still you may wonder about this prayer. Is it not a kind of deception, a self-delusion? Are things not fixed, for after all does God not work through the laws of nature which have long been fixed? Do we not also have to work for what we get? Why pray when we have to work for it? Are many things not just lucky breaks and the right pull? When facing such questions to remember, we must remember that we are responsible human beings. If the book is to be written, we must do the writing. If the field is to be harvested, we must do the seeding. God does not cripple us. He accompanies us and provides what we need. In praying the fourth petition we are also praying "give us today strength to earn our daily bread."

As we seek to reconcile the fourth petition with our uncertainties and questions, it may be wise to read again the Book of Job. Remember how Job lost all? Remember how the friends came and tried to explain why it happened? They only confused the issues. Job finally conversed with God. Their conversation revealed this: To fathom human suffering and existence is really beyond us. Job sees only a segment. He does not see the whole. Job's need is to recognize his humble status. He needs to meet life with a childlike trust, admittedly not knowing all or understanding much. He needs simple trust in God.

We may not understand how God answers, nor completely how our prayers influence God. We may not know how God works through laws of nature or through miracles. God has invited us to pray with childlike trust. And we have a deep need within us to pray.

Thinking of that, I am reminded of something clipped from a magazine years ago:

> A story goes that some fishes heard of a wonderful thing called water, and they swam about trying to find if anyone could tell them about this thing called water. Nobody knew. At last, a wise old fish made the revelation: They lived and moved and had their being in it. It was as near and as important as that.

As water is for those fish, so prayer is for us.

For your devotions

GIVE US today our daily bread

Psalm 145:15-19

Hymns: "We Plow the Fields and Scatter" and "He's Got the Whole World in His Hands"

Lord, as I look at the words "give us today our daily bread," I am taken aback by the bluntness of the request. Most of the time when I ask for something to be given to me, I cushion it with some explanation of why I am asking and seeking. In this prayer I bluntly ask for your handout to me. No games here, Lord; it is simply my life exposed—both the needs I have and my dependence upon you.

"Give us today our daily bread." O Lord, it is embarrassing to be asking. I come as a beggar. That seems demeaning. Yet, Lord, I must ask, for I am not sufficient in myself. I need you. I need what you offer. I am totally dependent upon you for the well-being of life—for its sustenance, its maintenance, as well as its meaning. Though I would like to think I am independent, it is not true. I am a dependent person—upon you and others too. So I come asking, seeking; sometimes I come in desperation, even pleading.

Lord, give. I am offering you nothing. I am at your mercy. I am depending upon you in your steadfast love and generosity to respond to me and my need. There is something in me that wants to declare my independence, but how can I rightfully claim that independence when I am to rely upon you for the answer to my every need in life? This petition, Lord, strips me of my boasts and exposes me to admit that I am as a child whose very existence is a gift and whose sustenance is gift upon gift.

Lord, I come saying, "Give." As I do, I admit that often when someone has asked me to give, I have resented being asked. I want to be the determiner of what and to whom I give. I tend to think those who ask have a lot of gall in their asking. Lord, this fourth petition of your prayer tempers my pride. I ought be more grateful for what you have given me. I ought to remember that I am your steward. I ought to live with open hand to others in need even as your hand is open to me in my need. I ought to quit priding myself in what I have. I ought to remember to be a servant rather than assume I am a master of my fate. Lord, I come with open hand to receive. Keep my hand open when there is opportunity to help. Amen.

Give us TODAY our daily bread

Matthew 6:25-34

Hymns: "Today Your Mercy Calls Us"
"I Know Who Holds Tomorrow"

Lord, you are the one and only security I have. I want security. Constantly I seek it. Frequently I fear to lose it. Only you are "the same yesterday and today and forever." How aptly You have shown this to me in the prayer your Son taught: "Give us today our daily bread." At first glance, the insertion of "today" in a petition requesting daily bread seems redundant to me. However, in further pondering the word "today," I'm reminded of my need to trust, to trust daily, for you are the source of all that answers my needs. You are my security. Lord, I would declare, "Begone with the worries and the needless meddlings which would give me only a false security." Lord, you are my all in all.

"Give me today." I need to pray that, Lord. I need to pray it so that I curb my selfishness. Greed is seeded in my life as I keep widening what I think I need, as I seek to satiate my desires. There is no satisfying me, for I have not learned like the apostle "in whatever state I am therein to be content." Instead I keep wanting and justifying the wants as if they were legitimate, lifesaving needs. I keep asking for bread, but really want cake. I keep moving to the fringes of what trusting you is, Lord, and sometimes I plunge off the edges of trust completely. Remind me again and again that you did not just teach me to pray, "Give us our daily bread." You teach me to pray, "Give us *today* our daily bread." Keep that *today* at the fore, Lord, so that I keep trusting you every day. Curb the misguided notions I have as to what I really need, so that sharing is a mark of my actions and servanthood is my mission. Spare me the tensions of living with a stockpile philosophy of life. Keep me aware that the life I live today is the vital *now*. Amen.

Give us today OUR DAILY BREAD

Luke 11:5-13

Hymns: "With the Lord Begin Your Task"
"God Will Take Care of You"

Lord, when I move from the "your" petitions to the "us" petitions in the prayer your Son taught, you surprise me. The "your" petitions have all been relational petitions, all dealing with my relation to you, the heavenly Father. I would have thought the "us" petitions would first have dealt primarily with my relationships to others, petitions dealing with what I think of as my spiritual relationships to people. I might have expected you, Lord, to *end* with the petition which brings me to the material and physical needs of life, to the work-a-day, making-a-living world. Instead, you invite me, right in the center of all the petitions, to think of my physical needs and to seek the answer to those needs.

Lord, this petition moves me to seek answers to questions.

Was it, Lord, that you wanted me to know that I am not going to get far in the emotional and spiritual development of life if I do not care for the physical factors?

Was it, Lord, that you knew I needed to rely on you for physical well-being if I really were going to have spiritual growth?

Was it, Lord, that you see need for me to know what are the necessities if I am to have the essential health and wholeness inherent in Your salvation?

Was it that you wanted me to stop separating the material and spiritual as if there were a chasm between them when in fact they intertwine in the daily expression of who I am?

Was it, Lord, that you want me to be bold in coming to you?

Was it that I should see you as God of all creation with an interest in the totality of creation and the complete well-being of each person?

Was it that I should be taking in gratitude rather than for granted?

Lord, you give me so much to ponder as I come asking you to give me my daily bread. Amen.

Forgive Us Our Sins, As We Forgive Those Who Sin Against Us

There is in every one of us an inward sea. In that sea there is an island; and on the island there is a temple. In that temple there is an altar; and on that altar burns a flame. Each one of us, whether we bow our knee at an altar outside ourselves or not, is committed to the journey that will lead him to the exploration of his inward sea, to locate his inward island, to find the temple, and to meet, at the altar in that temple, the God of his life. Before that altar, all the deepest intent of your spirit stands naked and revealed; before that altar, you hear the voice of God, giving life to your spirit, forgiveness for your sins, renewal for your commitment. As you leave that altar within your temple, on your island, in your inward sea, all the world becomes different, and you know that whatever awaits you, nothing that life can do will destroy you (Howard Thurman in *The Growing Edge*, Harper).

My father was killed by the Japanese during World War II. This incident caused me to harbor hatred which I kept even while I was in school preparing myself for service as a deaconess.

In February 1949, Dr. E. Stanley Jones came to Manila for a week of evangelistic services. I heard him speak every night. On the last day, he told the congregation he was going to Japan. He asked us if we were willing to make him our messenger for extending to the people there our message of love and forgiveness. If we were willing he requested us to raise the right hand.

I was in a dilemma. I wanted to remain loyal to the memory of my father. I also wanted very much to be true to Jesus' words. Others started raising their hand. Finally I was repeating the words: "Forgive us our trespasses as we forgive those who trespass against us." With tears of joy I eagerly raised my hand. From that moment my hatred and bitterness were changed into love and forgiveness (Philippine Deaconess Dorinda Umengam-Guillerons).

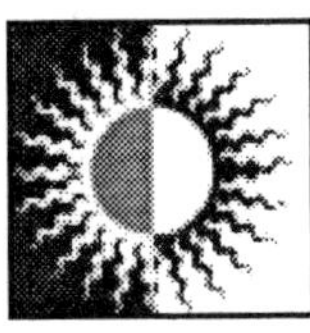

For your reflection

Taking Our Sin to God's Laundry

We cannot seem to agree what to call it. We do agree on what needs happen to it. In the contemporary version of the Lord's Prayer the word is "sin." In the traditional version it is "trespasses." In Malotte's vocal rendition it is "debts." All refer to the same thing, but in dealing with this phenomenon of human experience, there is no disagreement. We need and we seek forgiveness.

My bias is for the word "sin." The word "trespass" brings to mind some violation or disobedience. The word "debt" suggests something owed. The word "sin" covers all this and much more.

A parishioner in conversation with his pastor objected to the word "sin" being used in the fifth petition of the Lord's Prayer. He insisted that we sin only against God, and thus the word "sin" was not inclusive of what we seek when we ask for forgiveness. Perhaps he was thinking of Psalm 51:4a: "Against you, you alone, have I sinned, and done what is evil in your sight." Sin, indeed, is against God. What this parishioner overlooked is that what we do against God includes what we do against others and also what we do against ourselves.

The word "sin" in Hebrew usage of the Old Testament falls into at least four categories. 1) It is deviation from the right way (i.e., "missing the mark"). 2) It is guilt as opposed to innocence. 3) It is rebellion against a superior, or unfaithfulness to an agreement. All life is upheld by covenant. The essence of sin is its breach of that covenant. 4) The concept of sin also is conveyed by a wide variety of words such as violence, evil, destructiveness, trouble, worthlessness, vanity, folly, senselessness. "To act in opposition to life is to commit sin."

We come to God seeking forgiveness. To discern what you seek in forgiveness, think of something you have done to a member of your family which you feel may have hurt him or her. You go to that person, you confess what you did as wrong; you ask forgiveness. If the individual responds by shrugging his or her shoulders, saying, "Oh, that was nothing," you become aware that it really was not a matter of import and real hurt. On the other hand, if the individual hears you and then assures you that you are forgiven, two things have happened. First, the individual has accepted the hurt of your action and will bear it. Second, the individual will not let it stand between the two of you. It is past as far as the two of you are concerned in your relationship together.

To forgive someone is to take the hurt unto yourself and to release the guilty person so that there can be reconciliation and new life. That hurt we see our Lord taking as he dies on the cross, crying out, "Father forgive. . . ."

C. S. Lewis suggested that often what we seek is really not to be forgiven but to be excused. Lewis contrasted the two, noting that forgiveness says, "Yes, you have done this thing, but I accept your apology. I will never hold it against you, and everything between us two will be exactly as it was before." Excusing, on the other hand, says: "I see that you could not help it or did not mean it; you were not really to blame." If you are not to blame for what you did, then there is really no need for forgiveness.

Lewis pressed the point further:

> What we call "asking God's forgiveness" very often really consists in asking God to accept our excuses. What leads us into this mistake is the fact that there usually is some amount of excuse, some "extenuating circumstances." We are so very anxious to point these out to God (and to ourselves) that we are apt to forget the really important thing; that is, the bit left over, the bit which the excuses

> don't cover, the bit which is inexcusable but not, thank God, unforgivable. And if we forget this, we shall go away imagining that we have repented and been forgiven when all that has really happened is that we have satisfied ourselves with our own excuses. They may be very bad excuses; we are all too easily satisfied about ourselves.

I recall as a seminary student being asked in a homiletics class to go to the blackboard and to write the outline of a sermon which had been assigned. Feeling ill-prepared, I began to offer to the professor an excuse as to why I didn't feel my outline had merit. His quick response: "Marbury, if you have a reason, share it; if it's an excuse, we aren't interested." God knows all our excuses. In the fifth petition we are not dealing with God on the level of alibis. We are before God in admission of all the folly, failure, meanness, and shortcoming of our lives. We are seeking from God full and complete pardon. Nothing is hidden. Nothing is to be whitewashed by our own pretensions.

Forgiveness is the centerpiece of the Christian faith.

To be forgiven is to be a child of God. Forgiveness is like a cable linking us to the shore on the other side. Forgiveness is like a sentence pulling our lives together. Someone has said, "It is right to be concerned with our sins. It is wrong to be obsessed by them." Forgiveness is what can release us from this obsession. It is letting go, the release, the advent of the new.

What we have thus discussed is the vertical, our relationship with God. What about the horizontal, our relationship with one another? What happens for the person who says, "I will never forgive"? What effect does God's forgiving of us have on our readiness to forgive?

Robert Louis Stevenson, the poet, was living on one of the South Sea Islands. One morning, when leading family devotions, he got up in the midst of the Lord's Prayer and walked away. Because Stevenson was a man of frail health, his wife immediately became concerned. She followed him and asked what was wrong. Stevenson explained that the prayer had caught in his throat because of his unwillingness to forgive someone.

When Jesus taught us to pray "forgive us our sins," he also taught us to pray "as we forgive those who sin against us." That addition to the petition makes it sound as if God's forgiveness is contingent upon our forgiving. This is not true. There is, however, a link between being forgiven and being forgiving.

> Why is this so? Well, it is not because God waits for us to earn his forgiveness by forgiving others; we can never earn any of God's favors. It is simply because we cannot truly ask for forgiveness unless our heart is right regarding other people. God does not work by halves. He will not allow us to come to Him confessing half a sin while hanging on to the other half. It must be all or nothing. Thus, if we confess our sins, that confession must of necessity involve a forgiving attitude toward others (James Montgomery Boice).

We need forgiveness. Coupled with that need is the need to forgive. Our Lord, in teaching us to pray, lets us in on the secret that being forgiven and granting forgiveness are not two separate items in human experience. They interlink. In forgiving we open ourselves to forgiveness. As we forgive, God's grace flows through us to others and also to us. It is not an exaggeration to say, "The one sin which breaks fellowship with the Father is, 'I am not a sinner.'" We become aware of a related statement as we pray the fifth petition: "The sin which breaks fellowship with the Father is when we say, 'I will not forgive.'" God is the forgiving God. God's work in our lives is a forgiving work. The most Christian thing we can do is to forgive.

In 1977, Bishop Festo Kivengere, after the martyrdom of Archbishop Janani Luwum by Idi Amin in Uganda, realized his home was under surveillance. He realized he was a marked man. Though he hated so much to leave his Anglican diocese and his homeland, he found it advisable to flee. Writing about the experience in *Christianity Today*, Bishop Kivengere made these startling statements:

> I love Idi Amin. I have never been his enemy. I wish somebody would take that message back to him. If I were in Uganda, I would shout it from the housetops. If I could get near President Amin, I would tell him to his face. Actually, he knows it already.
>
> Is it surprising that I love him? It shouldn't be. This is a purely Christian response to the tragic events of recent

> weeks. It is not weakness, nor is it cowardice. Remember Christ and his response as he underwent that absolute injustice, being nailed to a cross. He didn't say, "Father, destroy them." No! He said, "Father, forgive them." Forgiveness is creative. Retaliation is destructive. Anyone who loves humanity must seek the constructive, reconciling way. God did it. Who am I to stray from His way? So that is why I love Idi Amin. Love can heal, and I will be committed to that until I die.

Into that spirit Jesus invites us as he teaches us to pray, "Forgive us our sins as we forgive those who sin against us." Jesus poured out upon the world his grace, his pardon, his forgiveness. What a benefit he was and is to the world! He invites us to pour out forgiveness upon this world. We, like him, can give a new spirit, a new freedom, a release from all the bitterness, the grudges, the ill will. We can open the door for new life through the things we do, the words we speak, the spirit and demeanor with which we live. "Forgive us our sins as we forgive those who sin against us." Life can be free of the failures and encumbrances of the past. Life is nurtured and strengthened in being forgiven and in being forgiving.

For your devotions

FORGIVE US our sin, as we forgive those who sin against us

1 John 1:5–10

Hymns: "Chief of Sinners Though I Be"
"Jesus, I Come"

Lord, I am guilty. I have sinned against you in thought, word, and deed. I have not loved others as I have loved myself. I have failed to meet the goals of my own life. Plagued by my sins and the evil in my life, I turn to you. The Scriptures declare, "The blood of Jesus his Son cleanses us from all sin." An old saint of the church is quoted as saying, "That's all I need, and I can't get along with less." I believe that, Lord. I turn to you. You are my one hope. Through your sacrifice for me you have shown your love for me. Through the death of your Son upon the cross you have made possible my reconciliation with you. In you is my forgiveness. I am clean again. My life is as a new slate upon which is to be written the new ventures of life lived in your love.

Lord, what a gift is the gift of your forgiveness! How it changes everything for me! Through forgiveness I am lifted out of the pit of despair upon the highway of right living. Through forgiveness I am sent forth to be a new person with the equipment of your gospel.

Lord, thank you for thinking of me. Thank you for sending your Son to open and enable the way of forgiveness. Thank You for sending the Counsellor to convict and convince me of my need for repentance and of your forgiveness. Thank you for release from my shame and shortcomings. Thank you for healing. Thank you, Lord, for being "the way, the truth, and the life." Amen.

Forgive us OUR SIN, *as we forgive those who sin against us*

Isaiah 1:18

1 John 2:1-2, 12

Hymns: "I Lay My Sins on Jesus"

"Cleanse Me"

Lord, there is one thing that stands in the way of right relationships and healthy living. That one thing is my sin. Sometimes it is called trespasses, for my sin is going where I am not supposed to be and doing what I am not supposed to do. Sometimes it is called debts because it is a failure to fulfill the rightful obligations I have. I prefer the word "sin," for to me it is an umbrella word that embraces all the ways in which I miss the mark; it is inclusive of all the evil that marks my existence and causes me to be misled and unresponsive to God's goodness. It denotes my shame. It designates the reason for my guilt. It indicates the entrapment of my life. It is my dis-ease.

I hate to admit it but it is true. I hide behind a mask trying to make an impression of being what I know that I am not. My life is a battleground. There are aspirations to the noble and good. But, like the apostle Paul, I also discover "I do not do the good I want, but the evil I do not want is what I do." In addition, there are times I find myself confused, wanting to do good but uncertain as to what the good really is—living it in varying shades of grey.

O Lord, forgive me, I pray. May my confidence in you be so great that I am not afraid to live. Rather, may I launch out with a firm resolve to be faithful, knowing that when I fail, you are there, ready to forgive and to send me forth again. May I tackle the problems of life with zest, even when it seems that I am being forced to compromise the ideal. May the right prevail in and through me. May the motives of my life, O Lord, be cleansed by your forgiving grace. May your forgiveness, not my sin, be the constant preoccupation of my thoughts, words, and deeds. Amen.

Forgive us our sin *AS WE FORGIVE THOSE WHO SIN AGAINST US*

Matthew 18:21-35

Hymns: "Forgive Our Sins As We Forgive"
"Lord, I Want to Be a Christian"

Lord, in teaching his disciples to seek your forgiveness, your Son taught them also to be forgiving. Help me to see the link between the two. In forgiveness is healing. To be healed I need to be healing. Otherwise I destroy the healing you give. In forgiveness is reconciliation. In being reconciled I need to be a reconciler. Otherwise I create rifts and cut off the possibilities of reconciliation. In forgiveness a constructive, redemptive work is taking place. Lack of forgiveness is destructive of human well-being. Rescue me, Lord, lest I destroy. Help me, Lord, to be involved where constructive forces are at work.

When you teach me to pray, "Forgive us our sins as we forgive those who sin against us," you open my life on both ends—toward You on the one hand, toward my neighbor on the other. My life cannot really be open unless it is open both ways. To have your forgiveness without forgiving whoever has wronged me would cause me to pollute your forgiveness with stagnant ill will that broods on wrongs and fails to let go of bitterness. To seek your forgiveness without resolve to be forgiving of the wrongs done to me is to overlook the immensity of the forgiveness I seek from you. It is to fill myself with self-pity. It is to have a false measurement of what has been done to me by weak and fallible human beings. It is to forget the debts I owe. It is to fail to remember that I am to look at others through the eyes of mercy and compassion.

Lord, I come seeking forgiveness. How great is the need for that forgiveness! I come also rejoicing that your forgiveness is as a spring welling up through me, touching favorably all with whom I am in contact.

"Forgive us our sins, as we forgive those who sin against us." Those words slipping across my lips make it sound as if I were saying, "Forgive, because I forgive." Everything in this prayer you have taught your people to pray, everything in your revelation of yourself through your Son runs contrary to that sentiment. your forgiveness is through your grace. Lord, I dare not think I am in a bargain with you. I dare not presume that forgiveness is some commercial enterprise. On the contrary, Lord, you have taught me to see that forgiveness is a gift that sets in motion a spirit running like a flowing stream. I am not to be the busy beaver damming up this spirit of grace and release. I am to let it flow. To experience it, to possess it is to share it. You have set in the world—and you seek to keep in the world—a whole new order for relationships. You have made clear that it is a spirit not of judging but of forgiving with which people are to live. Lord, thank you for setting in motion forgiveness. Keep it in motion through me. Keep it in motion when I am finding it especially hard to forgive. Amen.

Save Us from the Time of Trial

Wyn Blair Sutphin suggests in this petition we are in essence saying:

> Dear Lord, keep us from gambling with our souls. Don't let us take a flyer after every casual desire. Do not let us experiment with evil.

Thomas a'Kempis in *The Imitations of Christ* discusses the temptations Jesus faced in the wilderness and the temptations we face in life under four Latin words: *Cogiatio, Imaginatio, Delectatio, and Assensio.* First there is the thought which arises, *Cogiatio.* It may be prompted by an external suggestion. We bring this thought from the periphery into the center of our thinking forming a picture or image of it, *Imaginatio.* We keep gazing upon it and let our mouths water with delight, *Delectatio.* We actually fall when we assent to the suggestion and do it, *Assensio.*

> The tears of penitents are precious: a cup of them were worth a king's ransom. It is no sign of weakness when a man weeps for sin, it shows that he hath strength of mind; nay more, that he hath strength imparted by God, which enables him to forswear his lusts and overcome his passions, and to turn unto God with full purpose of heart (Charles Haddon Spurgeon).

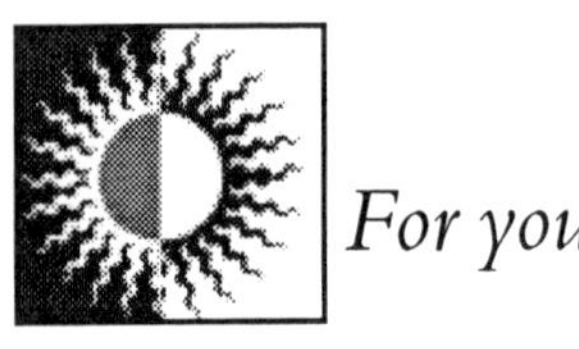

For your reflection

That We May Win

The sixth petition is perhaps the most difficult. A postgraduate student working for a doctorate in theology discovered this. He says,

> It was like one of those "Charlie Brown" experiences. You feel as though you don't have a chance—the kite won't fly, you'll never win the ball game, you're going to fail! I, the lonely candidate, was sitting on one side of the room. My thesis, which had taken months and months of my life to prepare, was laying on a little table in front of me. And ringed around me were the faculty examiners, ready to tear it apart and to prove that I didn't deserve the degree. I had prepared for this moment not only by thoroughly immersing myself in the subject matter but by learning some of the tricks of the trade. One thing you can do is try to get faculty members arguing among themselves. Well, the questions started coming at me, and the faculty members did some arguing among themselves. Then, like a bolt from the blue, the dean of the faculty cleared his throat and changed the subject. He asked me to explain the sixth petition of the Lord's Prayer. It caught me completely by surprise. It was not directly related to my thesis. And I gave what I knew was a totally unsatisfactory answer. When the examination was over, one of the faculty members took me aside and told me that the dean asked the same question of all doctoral candidates, regardless of the subject matter, and in his many years of experience on the faculty they had heard not one satisfactory answer (*Sunday Sermons*, Voicing Publications, February 20, 1983).

In more than four decades as a parish pastor I have had more questions regarding the sixth petition than any of the others. Apparently the biblical translators have had problems with an adequate translation. The King James and Revised Standard Version have the petition reading, "And lead us not into temptation." The New English Bible has it saying, "And do not bring us to the test," and the Jerusalem Bible, "And do not put us to the test." The new Revised Standard Version has Matthew 6:13 reading, "And do not bring us to the time of trial." The contemporary usage of the prayer has another slant for it has us praying, "Save us from the time of trial." Language is a fragile thing. Frequently we are uncertain regarding the best word and clearest expression.

Temptation and trials are moments of testing. We all face them. We are vulnerable. Suppose the lady's purse is open and you see money in it. You get the urge to take it. That is a moment of temptation, a time of trial. Suppose a lie is told about you. You hear about it and the person who spoke the lie is identified. You are tempted to get even. That's a time of trial.

> Yield not to temptation, for yielding is sin;
> Each victory will help you some other to win.
> Fight manfully onward, dark passions subdue;
> Look ever to Jesus, he'll carry you through.
>
> Ask the Savior to help you,
> Comfort, strengthen, and keep you;
> He is willing to aid you,
> He will carry you through.
> (Horatio Richmond Palmer).

That hymn of Sunday school days reminds of our Lord as a source of strength in the time of temptation. He is not the source of the temptation but helps in the defeat of the temptation. James in his epistle says:

> Blessed is anyone who endures temptation. Such a one has stood the test and will receive the crown of life that the Lord has promised to those who love him. No one, when tempted, should say, "I am being tempted by God"; for God cannot be tempted by evil and he himself tempts no one. But one is tempted by one's own desire, being lured and enticed by it; then, when that desire has conceived, it gives birth to sin, and that sin, when it is fully grown, gives birth to death (James 1:12-15).

James in those verses traces the history of sin from desires, dwelling upon the desire, yielding to the desire, and finally death. He also traces the history of the good life as desires, resisting the impulse to evil, and finally the crown of life. James makes clear, "No one, when tempted, should say, 'I am being tempted by God'; for God cannot be tempted by evil and he himself tempts no one." We cannot blame God for the temptation. A more subtle way of blaming God is suggested in this comment: "God created the heavens and the earth, man, trees, all other creatures, etc., and yet did not give man strength enough to resist temptation. Was man a faulty product? Surely Jesus was not faulty—maybe Adam should have been created strong like Jesus." Was Adam a faulty creation of God? Not if you read Genesis 2 and 3. God is not at fault for what happened to Adam and Eve. In the creation of Adam and Eve God did not create two more animals. God created Adam and Eve with the capacity to think, to choose, to decide. They were given free movement. They were created with capacity to be responsible for their actions. They were accountable. They were social beings. We are to see these abilities as great gifts that set us human beings apart. Unfortunately, we human beings misuse our special gifts. It's our fault that our lives are faulty. We cannot honestly, truthfully blame God. If we are to pray aright, we must recognize, as James did, that God is not the one who draws us to sin. He did not make us to be sinners. Sin is our fault as well as the fault of those around us. It is the result of the spirit of rebellion in the world against God.

The sixth petition is given for us to pray because we need God. We need God to protect us from our desires, from the spirit of rebellion that resides so often in us. We need God to prevail and to make us "more than conquerors" (Romans 8:37). God does not send the temptation and cause the trials. Even as we are not to put God to the test, it is doubtful that God puts us to the test. What then is God's will? St. Paul in 1 Corinthians 10:13 provides the answer:

> No testing has overtaken you that is not common to everyone. God is faithful, and he will not let you be tested beyond your strength, but with the testing he will also provide the way out so that you may be able to endure it.

We can expect the faithfulness of God. He is ready to help, to shut the gate of temptation, to provide a new and better way. God is not going to let us be "bowled over." Never can we really say, "I have no alternative but to succumb" in the face of sin. Never can we rightfully claim to be mere victims of circumstance. Never have we a right to self-pity and victimization as if our plight is impossible and there is no responsible door of escape. God will save us. God will give us the spirit of stubborn resistance to sin. God will provide a positive spirit and lead us forth to victory.

In Sir Walter Scott's *Bride of Lammermoor,* Bucklaw says of the devil:

> Whenever I am about to commit any folly he persuades me it is the most necessary, gallant, gentleman-like thing on earth, and I am up to saddle-girths in the bog before I see that the ground is soft.

Bucklaw is aware of deception. A man and a woman, for example, each became infatuated in someone other than their own spouses. They each got a divorce and then began immediately to make plans for a new marriage together. They went to the pastor to arrange a wedding. In conversation with the pastor they spoke of how they had prayed. They justified their divorces. They were sure all had happened because God had led them to do what they had done. Could it be they had been "up to the saddle-girths in the bog" without seeing "the ground is soft"?

When you walk with God in faith and commitment to him, there is the "necessary, gallant, gentleman-like thing on earth." Therein is repentance and forgiveness rather than the mere excusing of ourselves. In the walk with God comes the daily bread of concern, self-sacrifice, love, and service.

Charles F. Kemp in *Physicians of the Soul* shares the insights of Luther:

> He had a deep sympathy for those who were tempted, for he himself had been severely tempted. He said, "I have learned by experience how one should act under temptation." First he suggested that he should seek the comfort of the divine word and then the company of Christian people. He recognized the power of attention: "In these bodily temptations there is only one solitary way to over-

> come, namely, to turn away from the senses, the thought, and the heart; so also in spiritual temptations there is no other counsel, and no better help, nor more powerful remedy, than that one cast such thoughts out of his mind more and more, as best he can, and think upon the very opposite." He warned the tempted not to spend too much time alone with their thoughts, and said, with real insight, "If we are too much concerned for fear we may commit sin, we shall be overcome."

Luther faced head-on the trials and temptations. He saw them as tests to be passed. Luther lived dependent upon God and drew strength from the insights and support of the people of God.

> For our struggle is not against enemies of blood and flesh, but against the rulers, against the authorities, against the cosmic powers of this present darkness, against the spiritual forces of evil in the heavenly places. Therefore take up the whole armor of God, so that you may be able to withstand on that evil day, and having done everything, to stand firm. Stand therefore, and fasten the belt of truth around your waist, and put on the breastplate of righteousness. As shoes for your feet put on whatever will make you ready to proclaim the gospel of peace. With all of these, take the shield of faith, with which you will be able to quench all the flaming arrows of the evil one. Take the helmet of salvation, and the sword of the Spirit, which is the word of God (Ephesians 6:12-17).

There is a fascinating story behind Albert Durer's painting of the two hands clasped in prayer. Durer and a boyhood friend both had paintings entered in an exhibition. Durer's painting won the prize. The friend, of course, was disappointed that he had not won. In the disappointment he clasped his hands in prayer seeking strength to accept the second place with a generous spirit. Durer caught sight of his friend with his hands in prayer and painted what he saw. In facing trials and temptations you may find it beneficial to picture those praying hands—Durer's friend, his time of trial, his prayer! Rolling across your lips may there be the petition, "Save us from the time of trial."

For your devotions

SAVE US from the time of trial

1 Corinthians 10:6-13

Hymns: "If You But Trust in God to Guide You"
"If You Will Only Let God Guide You"

Lord, you are my Savior. To you I turn for saving power in the time of trial, in the hour of temptation. I must depend upon you to lead and guide me lest I forget and I forsake the way of truth and righteousness. You faced the evil one and showed the way of victory. In your love I too can be "more than conqueror."

Save me, Lord. What a prayer is in that word! It is terrible to be lost. It is glorious to be saved. In being saved is my health and wholeness. In being saved is the power of the gospel, leading me from faith to faith. In being saved, my faith is active in love. In being saved, I am ready to forget myself and to serve others. In being saved is hope, hope that brightens today and secures tomorrow. Save me, O Lord. It is everything to me and for me. It is life.

Help me, O Lord, not to fear the trials and dread the temptations that come my way. Rather, help me to face them with a confident spirit. You are with me and thus I need not fear. You have power greater than any of the ills of life. You share that power with me. Keep me humble, rejoicing in and receiving that power. You are the Good Shepherd who, when I follow, "leads me beside still waters," and "through the darkest valleys."

Lord, as I cry, "Save me," I know you are faithful and that you will "provide the way out." I will not fear the evil one who would thwart my understanding of the right and seek to destroy me. With you, O Lord, I will prevail, for you are my Savior. Amen.

Save us FROM THE TIME OF TRIAL

James 1:12-16

Hymn: "A Mighty Fortress Is Our God"

Lord, I am tempted—tempted to look after my own interests at the expense of others, tempted to give alibis for my actions so that I can evade responsibility, tempted to feel sorry for myself, thus justifying thoughts that are ignoble and motivated by evil, tempted frequently and in numerous ways. At these times of trial I am comforted, Lord, in knowing that you are never the source of the temptations and trials. I am comforted that you, too, faced temptations and trials when you were here on earth, thus letting me know you are familiar with what it is like to be human. I am comforted in the confidence that in "the hour of trial" you intercede for me. I am comforted in the assurance that in facing temptations and trials you will provide the way of escape and victory.

O Lord, sharpen my awareness of what is right and what is wrong. Energize my determination not to yield to temptation, not to succumb to evil. Strengthen my resolve for your will and kingdom. Convince me of your presence. Help me to see your light in the hours of darkness. Empower me that I may be an individual of integrity, character, and grace.

O Lord, in affirming my baptism I have promised "to live among God's faithful people, to hear his Word and share in his supper, to proclaim the good news of God in Christ through word and deed, to serve all people, following the example of our Lord Jesus, and to strive for justice and peace in all the earth." You have promised to save and redeem me. I believe that you do. Help me to live remembering what you have promised. Help me also to remember what I have promised. Lord, cause me always to turn my back upon "all the forces of evil, the devil, and all his empty promises." Cause me to go forth championing faith in you, putting my trust in you who are "able to guard until that day what I have entrusted to you." As Luther found strength in facing temptations asserting, "I am a Christian," so may I. When I am tempted, give me second thought—thought in which I remember what is right, what you will for my life. Lord, to go the way of temptation is to choose death. I would choose life. Amen.

Deliver Us from Evil

If I engage in prayer, then hope is born (Jacque Ellul).

I consider that the sufferings of this present time are not worth comparing with the glory about to be revealed to us. For the creation waits with eager longing for the revealing of the children of God; for the creation was subjected to futility, not of its own will but by the will of the one who subjected it, in hope that the creation itself will be set free from its bondage to decay and will obtain the freedom of the glory of the children of God (Romans 8:18-21).

Because you have made the Lord your refuge,
    the Most High your dwelling place,
no evil shall befall you,
    no scourge come near your tent.
For he will command his angels concerning you
    to guard you in all your ways.
On their hands they will bear you up,
    so that you will not dash your foot against a stone.
You will tread on the lion and the adder,
    the young lion and the serpent
    you will trample under foot.
Those who love me, I will deliver;
    I will protect those who know my name.
When they call to me, I will answer them;
    I will be with them in trouble,
    I will rescue them and honor them.
With long life I will satisfy them
    and show them my salvation (Psalm 91:9-16).

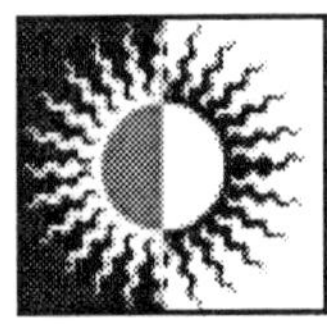

For your reflection:

Reverse Vision

According to a story, Martin Luther preached a sermon about attending to prayer. One of the rich farmers in his congregation after that service called him out and said, "Dr. Luther, do you see this horse? I'll give you this horse if you can pray the Lord's Prayer through once without your mind wandering." That was a very fine horse, so Luther summoned up all his concentration and said, "Our Father—by the way, does the saddle come with the horse?" By the time we come to the final petition of the Lord's Prayer, our minds have likely taken many side excursions, and we may not even be fully aware of what we are seeking. There is, however, even a more serious problem. Seeking deliverance from evil, are we fully cognizant of what evil is and the power it has upon us?

A clergy person tells of a child who had seen her teacher's new Revised Standard Version Bible. She went home telling her mother, "It's beautiful. It's the new Reverse Vision!"

That youngster may have had it more right than she knew. The Bible confronts us with a message that gives us a reverse vision. It's a vision quite reverse from the world and what the world would have us think concerning evil and the results of evil.

The apostle Paul writing to the church at Rome drew together a variety of Old Testament statements:

> There is no one who is righteous, not even one;
>   there is no one who has understanding,
>   there is no one who seeks God.
> All have turned aside, together they have become worthless;
>   there is no one who shows kindness,
>   there is not even one.
> Their throats are opened graves;
>   they use their tongues to deceive.
> The venom of vipers is under their lips.
> Their mouths are full of cursing and bitterness.

> Their feet are swift to shed blood;
> ruin and misery are in their paths,
> and the way of peace they have not known.
> There is no fear of God before their eyes
> (Romans 3:10-18).

Paul's readers must have been startled. As we look at that description of us and our existence, do we buy it or do we somehow seek to wiggle out from these indictments?

In recent decades there has emerged a tendency to soft pedal confession of sin in many services of worship. We seem uncomfortable owning up to the fact of sin and evil in our lives. A business executive credits some of his success in the business world to his acknowledgment of original sin. He insists that a failure to own up to the selfishness governing so much human behavior and action is to be naive and ineffective. He points to numerous instances in which negotiators of national tensions have failed in resolving those tensions because they have not dealt with the devious capacities and self-interest of leaders.

J. B. Phillips has said that the longer he has been a Christian, the easier he has found it to believe in the existence of the devil. Admitting there may be a devil makes more understandable his own capacity to sin and evil. Evil is real, and we need to admit the reality of evil. The apostle John put it this way:

> If we say that we have no sin, we deceive ourselves, and the truth is not in us. If we confess our sins, He who is faithful and just will forgive us our sins and cleanse us from all unrighteousness (1 John 1:8-10).

Our perception of the nature of evil may be sharpened in realizing evil is that which destroys us. Evil is that which leads to death, to our demise. Evil is that which thwarts the purposes of God. Evil is that which stymies God's purposes and ambitions. Evil is what the Ten Commandments forbid. Evil is the foreign element. Evil is the alloy in life. The cry in the seventh petition is a cry for purity.

The seventh petition links us to the first three petitions. We are delivered from evil as we hallow his name, ask for the coming of his kingdom, and do his will. The implications of the seventh petition are such as to revolutionize the whole course of life. God delivers us from evil so that we might be released for righteousness.

Our perception of the nature of evil may be sharpened in seeing evil as bondage. In Galatians 5 the apostle Paul lists works of the flesh (vv. 19-21) and fruits of the Spirit (vv. 22-23). His plea is that we live in the freedom which is in Christ and not sink back into the bondage of the flesh.

Within us is a tendency, an inclination in the direction of evil. We are not evil; we are the product of God's creative hand. Our lives are not evil; life is a great gift of God which is to be lived in its fullness and not lost to the evil forces. Evil is the rebellion. Evil is the tendency to be in rebellion to God. "Deliver us from evil" is not a cry to "deliver me from myself or from life." It is to cry for release from the forces which would imprison our lives. It is to pray that we might be free.

> Charles F. Andrews, the English missionary who was so great a Christian worker and servant of humanity in India that it was said his initials stood for Christ's Faithful Apostle, once told how his conscious, active life as a Christian began when he was eighteen. Though he had been brought up in a godly home, he was becoming indifferent to all religion and falling into sins that would ultimately have wrecked his character. One night, as he knelt to pray, came upon him an overwhelming realization of the holy presence of Jesus Christ. He struggled with a sense of his own evil life, and at last the voice of Christ seemed to bring forgiveness and love in place of darkness and despair. Andrews wrote later:
>
> Since that time, during more than 43 years of incessant struggle, journeying to and fro throughout the world, I have never lost the assurance of Christ's living presence with me. He is not a mere vision, He is no imaginative dream, but a living presence who daily inspires me and gives me grace. In him, quite consciously, I find strength in time of need (quoted by Jack Finegan in *Like the Great Mountains*, p. 54).

One of the things which I have found helpful in praying the Lord's Prayer is to associate with each petition events in the life of

Christ. It helps my concentration upon the petitions. It also widens the scope and content of the petitions. To pray the seventh petition recalling that Jesus cast out demons or to pray the seventh petition remembering how Jesus dealt with the woman taken in adultery or to pray the seventh petition thinking of how Jesus dealt with the Pharisees is to understand what deliverance from evil really is.

To pray the seventh petition, remembering how Jesus was tempted by Satan, is to recognize the subtlety of evil. That subtlety was illustrated by Sadhu Sundar Singh, who while in England wrote a friend in his homeland of India, "Pray for me because I am desperately tempted. I would rather spend all my time in prayer than go out and fulfill my engagements." To pray the seventh petition remembering Peter on the Mount of Transfiguration and his proposals for three booths is to understand how we may be evil even when we think we are good and wise. To pray the seventh petition in the light of Jesus' Sermon on the Mount in Matthew 5—7 is to penetrate closets of evil not only in our relationship but also in the inner secret chambers of our existence. To pray the seventh petition, hearing Jesus cry, "Father, forgive them; for they do not know what they are doing," may deliver us from the hang-ups which seed an unforgiving spirit within us.

The ultimate benefit of the seventh petition prayed with Jesus in mind is to recall resurrection morning. The final evil we face is death. Deliverance from evil in its final impact is deliverance from death. Jacque Ellul, the French scholar, was on target when he pointed out:

> The person who claims to be full of hope but fails to lead a life of prayer is a liar. Prayer is the sole "reason" for hope, at the same time it is its means and expression. Prayer is the referral to God's decision, on which we are counting. Without that referral there can be no hope, because we have nothing to hope for. Prayer is the possibility of God's intervention, without which there is no hope.

The seventh petition is the great resurrection petition. It is the petition which lets our lives blossom forth in hope. It is a petition opening us to God's intervention and victory.

An amateur radio operator will say, "Over," thus letting the other operator know it is his or her time to talk. The children of one amateur operator were excited about their father's involvement. They watched the procedure. They listened. One evening a young daughter of that operator ended her prayer saying, "Over," instead of "Amen." "And deliver us from evil. Amen." Over, Lord; take over.

For your devotion

DELIVER US from evil

Psalm 34

Hymns: "Guide Me Ever, Great Redeemer"
"Guide Me, O Thou Great Jehovah"

Lord, I come as one of the thieves on the cross the day your Son was crucified. I come seeking you to deliver me. I am held in the clutches of that which would destroy me. Set me free, Lord. Give me the confidence of release, release from all that is evil and release for all that is good. Help me to remember that your Son came to this earth to imprison all that would hold your people captive. I cry, "Deliver," knowing that I am delivered. "Make me a captive, Lord, and then I shall be free."

You set me free, Lord, for I bear the name Christian. Therein is my identity. Therein is my salvation. Let no one fool me. Keep me from searching for identity. Rather, cause me to rejoice in the identity you have given me.

You set me free, Lord, for I have a power. It is the power of the gospel unto salvation. Instead of looking for strength within, cause me, Lord, to draw upon the resource of power that is ever at my disposal. Give me trust in your miraculous power so that I go forth knowing there is a power working in and for me which is able to do more than I even dare ask or think.

You set me free, Lord, for even death has no hold upon me. I am on a pilgrimage. When "death's cold, sullen stream shall o'er me roll"

I need have no fear, for You will "bear me safe above." Heaven is my home. I look for the new Jerusalem, for you have given me a new faith "through the resurrection of Jesus Christ from the dead."

You set me free, Lord, for I am a member of your family. Your family is a family which can rejoice in suffering assured that "suffering produces endurance, and endurance produces character, and character produces hope, and hope does not disappoint" because your love has been poured into our hearts. I am delivered, O Lord, even as I cry, "deliver us from evil." Amen.

Deliver us FROM EVIL

Galatians 5:1, 16-26

Hymns: "Lord Jesus, Think On Me"
"Precious Lord, Take My Hand"

Lord, this world is "filled with woe and evil;" and my life is "prone to sin." I have the tendency to lament how evil this world is becoming. This preoccupation with evil, Lord, seems only to give excuse for the failings in my life and the pessimism which casts a color of gloom over the living of that life.

Lord, I come ever needing and asking you to deliver me from evil. Make me, I pray, understand the inner dynamics of evil in my life. The greatest sin is the sin which I fail to recognize as sin. Incline me to the Ten Commandments and a fulfilling of what they command. Purify the motives with which I act. Break the bonds of my rebellion. Snap the cord of death which the Destroyer seeks to place on me. Keep my personal piety an obedience to you and my worship a "worthship" of you, so that neither is a cover for a failure to pursue justice and peace. Give me an honest perspective of the moral chaos that spreads corruption. Help me to reject covetousness and love opportunity for service. I would not make light of the evil with which the devil, the world, and my own flesh inflict me. I would strongly rejoice in you, your gifts, and your salvation. Lord, in my life I believe you desire people to take precedence over things. I believe that things are to be received as a trust from you through which I practice good stewardship.

Lord, I would take up your whole armor that I may withstand the evil day and be able to "stand firm." Clad with "the belt of truth," "the breastplate of righteousness," the shoes of the Gospel, "the shield of faith," "the helmet of salvation," and "the sword of the Spirit," I would "quench all the flaming arrows of the evil one."

According to your word, Lord, I am cleansed, saved, and delivered. What powerful petitions and affirmations you place upon my lips! What joys you place within my life! What confidence you give to confront the issues of this day! Thanks be to you. Amen.

For the Kingdom, the Power, and the Glory Are Yours, Now and Forever. Amen.

The London branch of one of the great publishing houses of Great Britain is named the Amen House. Perhaps it was called that because, in the early days of the existence of the house, it was near St. Paul's Cathedral.

This is a good house to build—an Amen House! It does not mean a house where pious talk is on tap all the time or where holy amens are dropped all over the place. That would be something to run from—fast! Remember that Jesus rebuked this sort of pretense: "Not every one who says to me, 'Lord, Lord,' shall enter the Kingdom of heaven, but he that does the will of my Father who is in heaven" (Matthew 7:21).

The root meaning of amen is "so be it." To build an Amen House is to build a house and home in which the whole of the family says to the commandments of God and to the teachings of Christ, "So be it," and puts the prayer into action (Halford Luccock).

Amen comes from the Hebrew *aman*, which means "to nurse."

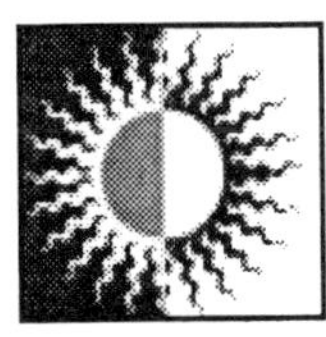

For your reflection

Our Doxology of Praise

The word "Amen," an ancient Hebrew word which may have been picked up from the Egyptian, came into common usage in the

Jewish synagogue during the days of the Babylonian captivity. It passed into the New Testament occurring, for example, 30 times in Matthew and 25 in John where it is translated "truly" and "verily," and has become a great word of the Christian vocabulary throughout the history of the Christian church.

Amen comes from a root which has the idea of firmness; it might be rendered as true, truly, certain, or certainly. It corresponds simply to the word "yes." We have an example of this where Paul writes: "For in him every one of God's promises is a 'Yes.' For this reason it is through him that we say the 'Amen' to the glory of God" (2 Corinthians 1:20).

As R. Martin-Achard points out, the word serves to

> confirm and support what has been said. By pronouncing it, the listener associates himself with what has been uttered; he recognizes it as valid, he makes it his own, he is ready to conform to it. Thus, Benaiah replied 'Amen' to the orders of David (cf. 1 Kings 1:36; Jeremiah 28:6). So, Amen is tantamount to a signature, to the giving of a promise... The people say 'Amen' to the commandments which Moses gives them, and by that they agree to follow them and they accept in advance the consequences implied (cf. Deuteronomy 27:15ff, 12 times; Nehemiah 5:13, Numbers 5:22).

The Amen in our prayers confirms our prayers. This is the great "yes." It is the great "so be it," but a "so be it" which carries firmness, truth, and certainty.

The Amen of the ascriptions of praise, of the doxologies in our worship, reveals the part we take in praising God. We are united in adoration and in invocation. The Amen underlies the importance and the truth of our prayers and our doxologies. The Amen to the declaration of our forgiveness is our expression of confidence, of trust, and of certainty. The Amen is our "yes" to God's "yes."

"And to the angel of the church in Laodicea write: The words of the Amen, the faithful and true witness, the origin of God's creation" (Revelations 3:14). Christ is the Amen of God to humanity. We respond in an Amen to him. No wonder there is the Amen of the people of God, also a note of hallelujah and praise as we see in Revelations 19:4. This element of praise as well as firmness is obvious in many points in the writings of the apostle Paul. (Examples are found in Romans 11:36, Galatians 1:5, and Philippians 4:20.)

Our God is the God of Amen (see Isaiah 65:16). We are a people of Amen (2 Corinthians 1:20). It is our business and our privilege as Christians to be firm and to be sure in a God who is firm and sure. Our response to God is our commitment in an Amen.

Permit me to suggest to you that the church is the Amen House. It is the house where the Holy Spirit of God convinces us of God's "so be it." It is the place where we respond with a "so be it" to God. The church is here as the great Amen House of God, so that your life will become a little Amen House. When God confronts us with his demands, we are to respond with an Amen. When God confronts us with his forgiveness, we are to respond with an Amen. When God confronts us with the hope of heaven, we are to respond with an Amen.

God looks for the Amen of our lips to be the Amen of our hearts. God anticipates that the Amen we speak is the Amen which is borne out of the conviction that "the kingdom, the power, and the glory" belong to God "now and forever." There cannot be a dual focus in our lives and an Amen. Yes is yes, not a mixture of yes and no.

The Lord's Prayer concludes on the note of praise. As a prayer of the heart and not simply of the lips, we conclude it is a doxology of praise and commitment.

It is possible to thank God without full commitment of life to God. There are always so many things for which to thank, so many reasons for expressing thanks. You cannot, however, praise God with a half heart. To praise God is to rejoice that God is God. This is taking God for what God is (not for what we want him to be) and rejoicing in him. We find thanksgiving easy when we finally get around to it. We find praise strange and sometimes even difficult. Thanksgiving calls for something from us. Praise calls for us. God's power is power for us. God's glory is our glory. But is it? Do we really want to be dethroned and let him rule? His power is resurrection power. He brings life out of death. Dare we believe that? His power is sanctifying power. He makes the unclean clean again. Dare we believe this as we look at our sin? God's glory is the glory in which we are to be content to live. Are we content to be overlooked as long as we know God gets the glory? An affirmative answer to these questions is the essence of praise. The whole of our being is involved in a doxology.

Somewhere I read an old story about brothers in a French monastery who were loved throughout the countryside for their loving service and kind deeds. None of them, however, could sing. Try as they may, the music of their service was a failure. The monks grieved over the fact that only in their hearts could they "make melody to the Lord."

One day a traveling monk stopped at the monastery. To the great joy of the monks, he was a wonderful singer. High, sweet, and clear, his voice rose over the other voices as they sang. One by one the others stopped and permitted him to do the singing.

That night in a dream an angel came to the abbot saying, "Why was there no music in your chapel tonight? Up in heaven we always listen for the beautiful music that rises from the services in your monastery; tonight we were sadly disappointed."

"Oh, you must be mistaken," cried the abbot. "Ordinarily we have no music that is worthy of your hearing, but tonight we had a trained singer with a wonderful voice. He sang with us and his singing was so sweet that we all stopped to listen. For the first time in all these years, the music was beautiful."

The angel smiled and said softly, "And yet up in heaven we heard nothing."

To the Pharisees and some of the scribes Christ had this to say: "Isaiah prophesied rightly about you hypocrites, as it is written, 'This people honors me with their lips, but their hearts are far from me; in vain do they worship me, teaching human precepts as doctrines.' You abandon the commandment of God and hold to human tradition" (Mark 7:6-8).

There is no credit in being identified as one of those Pharisees and scribes. Rather the Psalmist was worthy as he cried, "Bless the Lord, O my soul; and all that is within me, bless His holy name!" (Psalm 103:1).

As we give voice to the words of the conclusion of the Lord's Prayer, we participate in a great doxology. That doxology assures us "that such petitions are acceptable to our heavenly Father, and are heard by him; for he himself has commanded us to pray in this manner, and has promised to hear us. Amen, amen, that is, yea, yea, it shall be so" (Martin Luther in the *Small Catechism*).

To the simple request, "Lord, teach us to pray," Jesus responded with fewer than 70 words. This is a prayer for all. This is a prayer for every day. This is a prayer which takes on special meaning at great Christian holidays. This is a prayer prayed in the morning, at midday, and in the evening. This is a prayer prayed on the prairie and upon the mountaintop. This is a prayer that is relevant whether you pray it in your home or in the church. How thankful we are that it is so broad, so inclusive, so inexhaustible. How thankful that it covers all that can affect our lives. Nothing human is alien to it.

The daughter of Karl Marx was speaking to a friend one day, and the discussion turned to religion. Said the daughter, "I was brought up without any religion. I do not believe in God, but the other day in an old German book I came across a German prayer, and if the God of that prayer exists, I think I could believe in him."

"What was that prayer?" inquired the friend.

In response she started, "Our Father in heaven."

The Lord's Prayer is a great prayer. It opens life to communion with a great God. Amen.

For your devotions

FOR THE KINGDOM, the power, and the glory ARE YOURS, now and forever. Amen.

1 Chronicles 29:10-13

John 18:33-40

Hymn: "Lead On, O King Eternal"

Lord, my life has been conditioned in such a way as to let royalty evoke awe and adoration in me. You are the King of kings, the Lord of lords. Heaven and earth are your kingdom. As I come to you, I come in awe. I would lift a doxology of praise. No one is more deserving of praise than you.

Words somehow defy the exaltation that I wish to express as I pray. Earthly kings let their people down, but you never fail your people. Earthly kings come and go, but you reign forever and ever. Earthly kings have imperfections, but you are the perfect one. O Lord, I yearn to magnify and adore you.

Pondering the feelings that royalty evoke, I am reminded, Lord, of how much I learn of my faith relationship to you by paying attention to the human experiences I have. It is through faith I know someone else at the deepest level. It is likewise through faith I know you, Lord. Strengthen my faith. It is through contact with others my friendship grows and is kept intact. It is likewise through contact with you, Lord, that I become increasingly aware of your presence and blessing. Keep me praying and responding to you in worship. It is through doing for others that I have a feeling of purpose and value in life. It is likewise through obedience to you, O Lord, that your kingdom becomes the power of my life. Move me to be trusting and obeying.

Yours is the kingdom, Lord.
You invite me to prayer.

Yours is the kingdom, Lord.
    You in your grace share it with me.
Yours is the kingdom, Lord.
    I have need, need answered in your kingdom.
Yours is the kingdom, Lord.
    I worship and adore you.

Praise and thanksgiving to you, O King. My life would be forever a crescendo of praise. Amen.

For the kingdom, THE POWER, and the glory ARE YOURS, now and forever. Amen.

Isaiah 40:29-31,

Acts 1:8

Hymn: "How Great Thou Art"

Lord, you invite me to pray. With a confident spirit relying upon your power, I am invited to pray.

How I long for power to rectify the ills of the world. How I long for power to set straight the course of my life. How I long for power to undo the evil in which I am tempted to participate. You have that power. You invite me to tap into that power. Praise and thanks to you, O Lord, in opening the door to the blessings and the goodness of that power.

As I exalt in your power, I think of Paul to whom you indicated your "power is made perfect in weakness." Lord, thank you for that word. It keeps me from despairing in my weakness.

As I exalt in your power, I am reminded of a danger that lurks within me—the danger of misusing that power. I need my every petition to be born of humility in which I am resigned to a will that is higher and clearer than mine. I need you, Lord. Always I need you. I need to receive you and your power upon your terms, not upon my own. You are always right, and I am not. You are the creator who understands fully the creation. I do not. I need my life to be tempered with the cry, "Lord, have mercy."

As I exalt in your power, I am reminded of my need of consistency. I live moving between faith and doubt. Sometimes faith in you and your power seems so easy. At other times it seems so impossible. Sometimes I want to be moving onward as a Christian soldier. At another time I lag behind, losing heart, feeling unsure and insecure. Lord, I seek consistency. May "the assurance of things hoped for, the conviction of things not seen" prevail in my life always. I exalt in the mind that was in your Son, Christ Jesus, "who, though he was in the form of God, did not count equality with God a thing to be grasped, but emptied himself, taking the form of a servant, being born in the likeness of men. And being found in human form, he humbled himself and became obedient unto death, even death on a cross. Therefore, God has highly exalted him and bestowed on him the name which is above every name, that at the name of Jesus every knee should bow, in heaven and on earth and under the earth, and every tongue confess that Jesus Christ is Lord, to the glory of God the Father (Philippians 2:6-11). Amen.

For the Kingdom, the power, AND THE GLORY ARE YOURS, now and forever. Amen.

Romans 11:33-36,

Luke 2:14

Hymn: "Battle Hymn of the Republic"

Lord, I am restless. I am looking for something that will make my life special. I want recognition and acceptance, but even more than that I want to be distinctive. I want to be an achiever who leaves a special mark on this world, a legacy of achievement. I'm looking for success and glory. And here in the doxology of the prayer your Son taught, I am saying "the glory" is yours.

Lord, I forget that the specialness of life is to be found in and with you. The real glory is yours. Going your way, living life with you is the height of triumph. Lord, help me not to forget. Sanctify me in the holy, for therein is glory.

Lord, before your ascension you assured your followers, "I am with you always." That promise is precious. That promise holds your glory for me, for your presence with and in me is the glory. As I affirm "and the glory are yours," I am affirming your presence.

Lord, I suffer, but "the sufferings of this present time are not worth comparing with the glory about to be revealed to us." Thank you for the glory that awaits me. Thank you for the glory that attends me as I move toward that glory. Thank you for the glory that adorns the abundant life you gave me. Amen.

For the Kingdom, the power, and the glory are yours, NOW AND FOREVER. Amen.

2 Corinthians 6:1-2

John 3:16

Hymn: "O God, Our Help in Ages Past"

Lord, I think of heaven. In my thinking I am prone to think of it as another place. In so doing, I limit heaven. Likewise, I think of eternity. In this thinking I am seeing it as beginning a long time ago and being without end. Putting eternity in the context of beginning and end, I am limiting eternity. Lord, I seem locked into thought that is limited by space and time—within the space and time I live. I believe you would not have me live limited by space and time. You are more than both, and with You I am to find heaven and eternity. I am to live breaking out of that which limits, confines, and restricts life. For this, O Lord, I praise and thank you.

Now and forever you are Lord and Savior. Now and forever I am to trust and be confident. Now and forever I am in your kingdom, your power, and your glory. Now and forever I can come to you knowing you want me to come, that you will not turn a deaf ear. Now and forever I am to ask in your name, being assured that what I ask in your name I will receive. Now and forever, Lord, you are conqueror, and with you I shall conquer.

Our times are in thy hand.
O God, we wish them there.
Our life, our friends, our souls, we leave
Entirely to thy care.

Our times are in thy hand,
Whatever they may be,
Pleasing or painful, dark or bright,
As best may seem to thee.

Our times are in thy hand;
Why should we doubt or fear?
A Father's hand will never cause
His child a needless tear.

Our times are in thy hand,
Jesus, the crucified;
The hand our many sins have pierced
Is now our guard and guide.

Our times are in thy hand,
We'll always trust in thee,
Till we have left the weary land
And all thy glory see.
(William Freeman Lloyd)

Amen.

For the Kingdom, the power, and the glory are yours, now and forever. AMEN.

Psalm 106:48

Rev. 3:14, 7:12, 22:20

Hymns: "God the Father, Be Our Stay"
"Amen"

Amen, heavenly Father.

Amen to the holiness of your name.

Amen to the coming of your kingdom.

Amen to your will being done on earth as in heaven.

Amen to trusting you to provide for the daily needs of life.

Amen to your forgiveness and my living in forgiving relationship.

Amen to my being safe in the time of trial and victorious over temptation.

Amen to deliverance from all evil.

Amen, Lord, yours is the kingdom.

Amen, Lord, yours is the power.

Amen, Lord, yours is the glory and to you be the glory.

Now and forever. Amen.

Lord, my Amen is my signature to the petitions I have prayed. My Amen is expressive of the sincerity with which I have prayed and my confidence that you have heard me. My Amen is the period I would place marking each request of you, Lord, as conclusive and completed.

O Lord, with Luther I confirm, "As your Amen is, so has been your prayer." O Lord, the Amen I speak emerges from the inner core of my being. It is expressive of the deepest conviction of my heart. I would have it reach even into those arenas of which I am not now consciously aware. I would have my whole life be an Amen to you, Lord, an affirmation of your saving lordship.

Amen, Lord, to the school of prayer in which your Son has taught. Thanks to you for the prayer in which that schooling takes place. Thanks to you for the invitation to pray, the guidance in prayer, the intercession on my behalf, and the participation we have together in prayer. Amen, Lord. Over, Lord, take over. Amen.